National Security

Current Issues

ReferencePoint Press™

San Diego, CA

Other books in the Compact Research series include:

Drugs
Alcohol
Club Drugs
Cocaine and Crack
Hallucinogens
Heroin
Marijuana
Methamphetamine
Nicotine and Tobacco
Performance-Enhancing Drugs

Current Issues
Biomedical Ethics
The Death Penalty
Energy Alternatives
Free Speech
Global Warming and Climate Change
Gun Control
Illegal Immigration
Nuclear Weapons and Security
Terrorist Attacks
World Energy Crisis

National Security

by Stuart A. Kallen

Current Issues

ReferencePoint Press™

San Diego, CA

For more information, contact
ReferencePoint Press, Inc.
PO Box 27779
San Diego, CA 92198
www.ReferencePointPress.com

Picture credits:
AP/Wide World Photos, 16
Maury Aaseng, 36–39, 53–56, 70–73, 87–90
United States Navy, 11

Series design:
Tamia Dowlatabadi

LIBRARY OF CONGRESS CATALOGING-IN-PUBLICATION DATA

Kallen, Stuart A., 1955–
    National security / by Stuart A. Kallen.
      p. cm. — (Compact research series)
    Includes bibliographical references and index.
    ISBN-13: 978-1-60152-020-3
    ISBN-10: 1-60152-020-4
    1. National security—United States. 2. Terrorism—United States—Prevention. I. Title.
    UA23.K297 2007
    355'.033073—dc22
                                                                      2007001567

Contents

Foreword

❝ **Where is the knowledge we have lost in information?** ❞

—"The Rock," T.S. Eliot

As modern civilization continues to evolve, its ability to create, store, distribute, and access information expands exponentially. The explosion of information from all media continues to increase at a phenomenal rate. By 2020 some experts predict the worldwide information base will double every 73 days. While access to diverse sources of information and perspectives is paramount to any democratic society, information alone cannot help people gain knowledge and understanding. Information must be organized and presented clearly and succinctly in order to be understood. The challenge in the digital age becomes not the creation of information, but how best to sort, organize, enhance, and present information.

ReferencePoint Press developed the Compact Research series with this challenge of the information age in mind. More than any other subject area today, researching current events can yield vast, diverse, and unqualified information that can be intimidating and overwhelming for even the most advanced and motivated researcher. The Compact Research series offers a compact, relevant, intelligent, and conveniently organized collection of information covering a variety of current and controversial topics ranging from illegal immigration to marijuana.

The series focuses on three types of information: objective single-author narratives, opinion-based primary source quotations, and facts and statistics. The clearly written objective narratives provide context and reliable background information. Primary source quotes are carefully selected and cited, exposing the reader to differing points of view. And facts and statistics sections aid the reader in evaluating perspectives. Presenting these key types of information creates a richer, more balanced learning experience.

For better understanding and convenience, the series enhances information by organizing it into narrower topics and adding design features that make it easy for a reader to identify desired content. For example, in *Compact Research: Illegal Immigration*, a chapter covering the economic impact of illegal immigration has an objective narrative explaining the various ways the economy is impacted, a balanced section of numerous primary source quotes on the topic, followed by facts and full-color illustrations to encourage evaluation of contrasting perspectives.

The ancient Roman philosopher Lucius Annaeus Seneca wrote, "It is quality rather than quantity that matters." More than just a collection of content, the Compact Research series is simply committed to creating, finding, organizing, and presenting the most relevant and appropriate amount of information on a current topic in a user-friendly style that invites, intrigues, and fosters understanding.

National Security
at a Glance

National Security

National security involves coordinating military, economic, diplomatic, and political power in ways that benefit the nation as a whole.

Terrorists

Islamic extremists consider it their religious duty to kill as many American men, women, and children as possible.

Threats

Terrorists may attack with conventional weapons, nuclear weapons, bioweapons, chemical weapons, or cyberweapons.

Bioweapons

A successful biological attack can threaten national security in several ways, causing mass panic, high casualties, and widespread economic disruption.

Foreign Oil

A war with Iran could cut Middle East oil production and send gas prices over $10 a gallon, creating a major economic depression.

The Patriot Act
The Patriot Act strengthens criminal penalties against terrorists and enhances government powers to conduct surveillance against suspects.

Privacy Rights
The National Security Agency has wiretapped thousands of Americans without the judicial warrants required for such activities.

The Bush Doctrine
The Bush Doctrine states that the government will defend the United States and the American people at home and abroad by identifying and unilaterally destroying any threats.

Iraq War
Between March 2003 and March 2007 the Iraq War cost American taxpayers approximately $400 billion.

Overview

66 National security . . . is the ability to preserve the nation's physical integrity and territory; to maintain its
economic relations with the rest of the world on rea-
sonable terms; to protect its nature, institutions, and
governance from disruption from outside; and to control its borders. 99

—Harold Brown, *Thinking About National Security.*

66 We seek to use America's diplomatic power to help
foreign citizens to better their own lives, and to build
their own nations, and to transform their own futures.
. . . Like the great changes of the past, the new efforts
we undertake today will not be completed tomorrow.
. . . But it is urgent work that cannot be deferred. 99

—Condoleeza Rice, "Transformational Diplomacy."

The concept of national security is invoked by politicians, pundits,
talk-show hosts, and average citizens on a daily basis. Because the
term is so all-encompassing it is used when discussing everything
from domestic terrorism to the Iraq War to trade policy with China. And
throughout American history, national security has involved dozens of
complex issues that include coordinating military, monetary, diplomatic,
and political power in ways that are beneficial to the nation as a whole.

A New York City firefighter takes a moment to look at the rubble of the World Trade Center, which was destroyed by terrorists on September 11, 2001.

In order to insure national security, the government must act on two broad fronts, formulating both foreign policy and domestic policy. Since new challenges develop all the time, those in charge of protecting national security must simultaneously deal with present problems and work to prevent future crises. Because of the uncertainties inherent in an unpredictable world, matters of national security are the motivating force behind a large percentage of decisions made by the federal government.

National Security and Diplomacy

To insure national security in the sphere of foreign policy, diplomacy has long been used as the first step toward fostering cooperation among allies and controlling the actions of hostile nations. Diplomatic matters are coordinated by the secretary of state, who oversees the State Department. This cabinet-level national security office employs thousands of people who represent U.S. interests abroad and work in U.S. embassies in almost every nation in the world. Members of the diplomatic corps within the State Department conduct international relations concerning war, peace, culture, economics, and trade. And diplomats negotiate and write countless international treaties that are endorsed by Congress and signed by presidents.

> **Throughout American history, national security has involved dozens of complex issues that include coordinating military, monetary, diplomatic, and political power in ways that are beneficial to the nation as a whole.**

The ongoing, complex national security work conducted by diplomats within the State Department is astounding. On a single day in February 2007, the State Department moved to resolve disputes between Palestinians and Israelis, signed a nuclear nonproliferation agreement with North Korea, and attempted to negotiate a peaceful settlement between warring factions in Iraq. This was in addition to less pressing national security matters such as negotiating oil leases in Cyprus and working to institute a peaceful political process in Somalia.

The National Security State

Diplomats in the United States operate with the knowledge that their negotiations are backed by the most powerful military force in the world, and the Department of Defense (DOD) is the branch of government called upon when diplomacy fails. Operating out of the Pentagon, DOD coordinates policy for the U.S. Army, Navy, Air Force, and Marines while consuming about half of the entire federal budget every year—an amount of money equal to the military budgets of all other countries in the world combined. This gives the United States what is called "power projection," or the ability to affect world events by threatening military force—or using force—in distant lands.

Power projection has played a large role in national security since the end of World War II when the Soviet Union (USSR) and the United States were left with the two largest standing armies in the world. In the years that followed the war, the United States maintained its power by building tens of thousands of nuclear weapons and intercontinental ballistic missiles (ICBMs) in order to prevent the Soviets from taking over Western Europe and small nations throughout the world. The USSR answered by projecting their own power in a similar manner and a nuclear arms race ensued for nearly 40 years. During this time the United States spent trillions of dollars building the most complex national security apparatus in the world.

> " Operating out of the Pentagon, [the Department of Defense] coordinates policy for the U.S. Army, Navy, Air Force, and Marines while consuming about half of the entire federal budget every year—an amount of money equal to the military budget of all other countries in the world combined. "

During the Cold War, branches of the government charged with protecting national security grew to include the Departments of Justice and Energy along with dozens of smaller agencies, including the Defense Intelligence Agency (DIA), the National Security Agency (NSA), the Central Intelligence Agency (CIA), and the Federal Bureau of Investigation (FBI). Except for the FBI, these agencies were coordinated, essentially, to fight a single conflict—the Cold War between the United States and the Soviet Union. And for more than 40 years U.S. power projection kept Soviet expansionism in check, and nuclear war was prevented.

A New World Order

While the Cold War was a long, complex, and costly conflict, the enemy was recognizable and victory easy to measure—most Americans believed that if the United States defeated a single nation, the Soviet Union, national security would be ensured. In 1991 this dream became reality when the Soviet Union was dissolved and re-formed as the democratic Commonwealth of Independent States. In his 1991 State of the Union address, president George H.W. Bush commemorated the occasion, envisioning "a new world order, where diverse nations are drawn together in common cause to achieve the universal aspirations of mankind: peace and security, freedom, and the rule of law."[1]

> **Unlike the monolithic Soviet Union, there seems to be no hope of defeating [terrorists] or negotiating peace treaties to stop their mission.**

In the decade that followed, the importance of national security seemed to diminish. Less money was devoted to the armed forces and intelligence agencies charged with rooting out threats of espionage. In fact, on September 10, 2001, Attorney General John Ashcroft proposed massive budget cuts for the Federal Bureau of Investigation's counterterrorism division, a branch of the FBI charged with preventing terrorist attacks. According to journalist Matthew Brzezinski, Ashcroft believed "the United States did not need a vast counterterror apparatus. It was a waste of time and money to develop expensive expertise in a fringe area that had so little impact on American everyday life."[2]

The next day 19 terrorists hijacked jetliners and slammed them into the Pentagon and World Trade Center towers and crashing another plane into a field in Pennsylvania, killing nearly 3,000 people. In the weeks following these tragic events it became clear that Americans were no longer guaranteed personal safety on U.S. soil. Suddenly, upgrading and improving the national security apparatus was urgently needed, as never before in history, to defend American interests abroad while also protecting homes, businesses, and offices in the United States.

America's new enemy is unlike anything ever encountered. Armed with computers, small weapons, and knowledge of terrorist tactics, they are anonymous suicidal individuals who work for small terrorist organizations. Their main mission is to kill as many American men, women, and children as possible. Unlike the monolithic Soviet Union, there seems to be no hope of defeating them or negotiating peace treaties to stop their mission. The power projection of the United States is useless against this new threat.

The Department of Homeland Security

In the aftermath of 9/11, government officials were forced to reconfigure their definition of national security to encompass the domestic United States. As Cynthia A. Watson writes in *U.S. National Security:*

> Homeland security is an aggressive, active movement to prevent any sort of terrorist activity from ever occurring in the homeland. Homeland security moves actively to build the strongest, most comprehensive network of antiterrorist policies and pursues them in a much more deliberate, calculated manner. . . . [Homeland] security requires defense of our territory and way of life from outside forces, through the coordination of all instruments and organizations of national power (both governmental and private).[3]

In order to coordinate this new national security mission, Congress passed the Home-

> " The [Department of Homeland Security] must defend the national security of the United States by preventing or responding to terrorist attacks carried out with conventional weapons, nuclear weapons, bioweapons, and cyberweapons. "

land Security Act of 2002, which created the Department of Homeland Security (DHS). As a result of this change, dozens of federal agencies, such as the Immigration and Naturalization Service, the Transportation Security Administration (TSA), the Secret Service, and the Coast Guard have become part of the DHS. As overseer of the department, the director of DHS, or the "Homeland Security Czar," is instructed to follow the mandate written by Congress:

> The mission of the Office will be to develop and coordinate the implementation of a comprehensive national strategy to secure the United States from terrorist threats or attacks. The Office will coordinate the executive branch's efforts to detect, prepare for, prevent, protect against, respond to, and recover from terrorist attacks within the United States.[4]

To carry out its mission the DHS must defend the national security of

A container ship is docked at the Georgia Port Authority Garden City Terminal in Savannah, Georgia. Security experts fear that terrorists may be actively plotting to attack U.S. ports.

the United States by preventing or responding to terrorist attacks carried out with conventional weapons, nuclear weapons, bioweapons, and cyberweapons. While doing so the department must protect millions of vulnerable targets, including airports, financial centers, power stations, ports, rail lines, chemical factories, telecommunications systems, government buildings, roads, and even farms and food-processing plants. The department has spent about $50 billion a year on national security since 2003.

Gathering Intelligence on Americans

Since it is impossible to guard and protect such a wide range of disparate targets, the government has initiated a series of programs designed to gather intelligence about possible terrorist attacks. Using the high-tech surveillance systems of the NSA, government agents have looked for suspicious individuals by investigating the private records of millions of U.S. citizens. In addition, the Patriot Act, passed by Congress in October 2001and reauthorized in 2006, gives law enforcement authorities expanded powers to act against would-be terrorists, including conducting secret investigations of individuals.

> " **Government agents have looked for suspicious individuals by investigating the private records of millions of U.S. citizens.** "

Under provisions of the Patriot Act, to expose possible terrorist activity authorities may search personal records, including bank statements, Internet search histories, medical files, and even records of videos rented and books checked out of the library. The Patriot Act also allows secret searches of a person's home and property without a search warrant. During such "sneak and peek" operations, agents may take personal papers and property without ever notifying the suspect.

Many provisions of the Patriot Act have generated bitter criticism from civil libertarians, who say that it is unconstitutional to allow authorities to investigate Americans without probable cause. Some of the programs, such as warrantless wiretapping, have been challenged successfully in court. Others, such as the investigation of private records, have been deemed constitutional.

Enemy Combatants and National Security

Beyond investigatory power, the George W. Bush administration has pursued other controversial matters in the name of antiterrorism and national security. On November 13, 2001, President George W. Bush issued a military order that denied suspected terrorists the legal protections of the U.S. criminal justice system. Called "Detention, Treatment, and Trial of Certain Non-Citizens in the War Against Terrorism," the order grants sweeping powers to the military to arrest, detain, and put on trial anyone suspected of committing terrorism against the United States, its citizens, its national security, foreign policy, or economy.

> "To expose possible terrorist activity authorities may search personal records, including bank statements, Internet search histories, medical files, and even records of videos rented and books checked out of the library."

In the weeks after the order was issued, Bush declared that as commander in chief he had the right to label any suspect an enemy combatant, even a U.S. citizen. And anyone so labeled could be held indefinitely by the military with no access to the criminal justice system. Enemy combatants could also be denied a military trial if it was believed that such a trial would compromise national security by revealing top secret plans, military maneuvers, undercover agents, or other covert information.

Enemy combatants granted a trial before a military tribunal face a system that operates much differently, with much more permissive rules regarding evidence, than the American legal system. Unlike civilian courts, prosecutors at tribunals may introduce evidence that is obtained under duress. This type of evidence is considered unreliable by the criminal justice system because it may be coaxed out of the defendant or witnesses through extreme interrogation methods or torture. Tribunals can also introduce evidence that is kept secret from the defendant and his lawyer, which makes it harder for the defendant to refute the charges. The tribunals themselves may be held in secret without access granted to the press, public, or relatives of the defendant. And once a judgment is rendered, there is an extremely limited appeals process.

Spreading Democracy

Officials are not relying only on punitive measures to stop terrorism. Many within the government believe that the best way to ensure national security is to bring education, improved living conditions, and justice to impoverished lands. This is meant to counter the conditions of poverty, unemployment, and authoritarianism in Muslim nations that help terrorist organizations find new recruits. As *The 9/11 Commission Report* states, terrorists blame the United States for their problems and believe "America is . . . responsible for the [repressive] governments in Muslim countries"[5]

To counter these feelings, some believe that the best way to fight terrorism is to bring democracy to the Middle East. As Bush stated in a March 2005 speech:

> By now it should be clear that decades of excusing and accommodating tyranny, in the pursuit of stability, have only led to injustice and instability and tragedy. It should be clear that the advance of democracy leads to peace, because governments that respect the rights of their people also respect the rights of their neighbors. It should be clear that the best antidote to radicalism and terror is the tolerance and hope kindled in free societies. And our duty is now clear: For the sake of our long-term security, all free nations must stand with the forces of democracy and justice that have begun to transform the Middle East.[6]

> "Bush declared that as commander in chief he had the right to label any suspect an enemy combatant, even a U.S. citizen."

While few could argue with the president's idealism, a contentious national debate erupted over whether such a mission is possible. Bush has often cited the need to spread democracy in the Middle East as his rationale for invading Iraq in March 2003, and at the time of the president's speech Iraq had held several democratic elections and adopted a constitution. However, democracy was doing little to solve Iraq's problems, and the country remained embroiled in violence, chaos, and sectarian bloodshed.

> **Many within the government believe that the best way to ensure national security is to bring education, improved living conditions, and justice to impoverished lands.**

By 2007 Iraq was engulfed in a full-scale civil war, and nearly two-thirds of Americans were demanding a withdrawal of U.S. troops. Many who opposed the war argued that it was a distraction that was actually weakening U.S. national security and that the United States could not continue to spend $2 billion a week to bring democracy to a nation that did not want it. In addition, the war had put such a severe strain on the American military that it could not adequately respond to threats from other hostile nations such as North Korea or Iran. The president's supporters countered that while it may take decades to bring democracy to Iraq, in the long run, victory would guarantee U.S. national security.

Oil Dependency and National Security

Whatever the arguments about democracy, the Middle East remains extremely important to U.S. security interests because 20 percent of the oil used by Americans is imported from that region. Cheap oil is the lifeblood of the American economy, and government planners say that any disruption in the flow of that oil to the United States would constitute a major threat to the United States. As an example, the CIA states that a war with Iran could cut Middle East oil production and supplies and send gas prices over $10 a gallon in a matter of weeks, creating an economic depression unlike any seen since the 1930s.

Because of oil's importance, former CIA director John Deutch and former secretary of defense James R. Schlesinger compiled a report for the Council of Foreign Relations called "National Security Consequences of U.S. Oil Dependency." The report states that the United States has long made a strategic mistake by treating energy policies as separate and distinct from national security policies:

The lack of sustained attention to energy issues is undercutting U.S. foreign policy and U.S. national security. Major energy suppliers . . . have been increasingly able and willing to use their energy resources to pursue their strategic and political objectives. Major energy consumers—notably the United States . . . are finding that their growing dependence on imported energy increases their strategic vulnerability and constrains their ability to pursue a broad range of foreign policy and national security objectives. The challenge over the next several decades is to manage the consequences of unavoidable dependence on oil and gas . . . and to begin the transition to an economy that relies less on petroleum. The longer the delay, the greater will be the subsequent trauma. For the United States, with 4.6 percent of the world's population using 25 percent of the world's oil, the transition could be especially disruptive.[7]

The National Security Calculus

Oil, economics, terrorism, and war pose major questions about U.S. national security in the twenty-first century. However, with more than 300 million people living in the United States, little clear-cut agreement exists over how to deal with these issues. In order to pursue any policies, officials not only have to work within the Constitution but also satisfy the demands of a diverse cultural and political society. As Cynthia A. Watson writes:

> Because the United States has such well-established democratic traditions . . . not even the fears of vulnerability to global and insidious terrorism can make us abandon the checks and balances that we both cherish and take for granted. At the same time, the various social forces that believe they deserve a voice in the

> **Many who opposed the [Iraq] war argued that it was a distraction that was actually weakening U.S. national security.**

formulation of national security policy are wide-ranging and often surprising. Within the field, the term "national security calculus" is often used to describe the balance between the threats facing our country, the tools available to defend against them, the freedoms and openness required by our democracy, and the various political and social interests and other variables that may enter the decision-making process. National security decision making is not, however, a mathematical equation wherein one side equals the other in precise, even terms. It involves weighing the various elements and identifying the best-case options. Every single calculation includes victories and losses; nothing that a national security strategist does is without costs of some sort.[8]

Whatever the costs, it is the job of countless politicians, administrators, researchers, and military planners to protect the national security of the United States on a nearly infinite number of fronts. These people work behind the scenes day after day to ensure Americans are safe, secure, and maintain their personal liberty.

How Serious a Threat Is Terrorism to National Security?

66 **America is at war with a transnational terrorist movement fueled by a radical ideology of hatred, oppression, and murder.**99

—George W. Bush, "Overview of America's National Strategy for Combating Terrorism."

66 **One of the remarkable things about September 11 is that there was no follow up—no shopping malls were firebombed, no bridges were destroyed, no power plants assaulted. . . . [This] represents a lack of wherewithal on the part of would-be terrorists.**99

—Luke Mitchell, "A Run on Terror."

The terrorist attacks on September 11, 2001, dramatically reminded Americans that the nation could be threatened by suicidal terrorists operating within the borders of the United States, and the attacks emphasized recent trends in international terrorism. According to U.S. intelligence experts, the 9/11 strikes came not from a single state-sponsored group as they might have in previous years, but from a loose affiliation of Islamic extremists. The attacks were also global in scale, plotted over the course of two years by terrorists from Yemen and Saudi Arabia who trained in Afghanistan. While living in Europe and the United States the terrorists used the Internet and cell phones to communicate and raise approximately $500,000 to pay for the attacks.

The strikes showed a shift in focus from traditional terrorist operations. Whereas in past years terrorists largely targeted military and government facilities and personnel, they were now able to terrorize entire populations by inflicting massive civilian casualties. According to FBI counterterrorism director Dale L. Watson, "These trends underscore the serious threat that international terrorists continue to pose to . . . the United States."[9]

Domestic and International Terrorists

There are two types of terrorist threats facing the United States: domestic and international. Domestic terrorism is the unlawful use or threatened use of violence by individuals or groups based within the nation's borders. These terrorists operate without direction or influence from foreign entities. One example is right-wing radical Timothy McVeigh, who was convicted of bombing the Alfred P. Murrah Federal Building in Oklahoma City on April 19, 1995, killing 168 people. Like all terrorists, McVeigh was politically, not financially, motivated. He destroyed a government building because of racist and antigovernment political philosophies.

> **There are two types of terrorist threats facing the United States: domestic and international.**

The Oklahoma City bombing represents the deadliest act of domestic terrorism in U.S. history. Since 9/11, however, national security experts believe a larger threat looms from international terrorists attempting to carry out operations against U.S. interests. According to Dale L. Watson's testimony before Congress, "International terrorism involves violent acts or acts dangerous to human life that are . . . intended to intimidate or coerce a civilian population, influence the policy of a government, or affect the conduct of a government."[10]

A Global Jihad

The powerful Islamic militant Osama bin Laden is a prime example of an international terrorist. Bin Laden issued a declaration of war, or fatwa, against the United States in February 1998, declaring that Muslims should consider it their holy duty to kill any Americans, anywhere on earth. In separate statements, according to *The 9/11 Commission Report,* Bin Laden called himself the messenger of God and "the organizer of a new kind of war to destroy America and bring the world to Islam."[11] Since Bin Laden made those pronouncements thousands of followers have dedicated themselves to carrying out his fatwa. They violently oppose Americans and believe that the United States and European powers have stolen the land and oil wealth of the Middle East while corrupting its culture.

In addition to Bin Laden's followers, a new generation of terrorists has emerged since the United States invaded Iraq in March 2003. In December 2004 the National Intelligence Council (NIC), a think tank run by the Central Intelligence Agency, analyzed the work of 16 government spy services and published a stark evaluation of terrorist threats called "Report of the National Intelligence Council's 2020 Project." It states that hatred of the United States, caused by the invasion of Iraq, has inspired radical jihadists, or those who fight for Islam, to wage war against Americans. In the language of the study, the Iraq war has provided "recruitment, training grounds, technical skills and language proficiency for a new class of terrorists who are 'professionalized' and for whom political violence becomes an end in itself." These terrorists will spread out around the globe seeking revenge in Europe, North America, and elsewhere. Major cities in the United States in particular face "an increasing risk of an attack involving biological agents, such as anthrax, and . . . chemical weapons."[12]

Because of such pronouncements, security experts believe that a deadly attack on U.S. soil within the next five to 10 years is likely. What is not assured is that such an attack, no matter how horrific, would threaten the ability of the United States to maintain its status as a world power. As Luke Mitchell writes in *Harper's:* "Although there may be no

> " Bin Laden issued a declaration of war, or fatwa, against the United States in February 1998, declaring that Muslims should consider it their holy duty to kill any Americans, anywhere on earth. "

shortage of those angry enough to commit acts of violence against the United States, few among them possess the training, financing, or the sheer ambition necessary to execute an operation [that would threaten national security]."[13]

Do Bioweapons Threaten National Security?

Although U.S. intelligence agencies say that terrorists might use biological weapons within the United States, debate is considerable over how threatening such an attack might be to national security. Bioweapons such as anthrax, smallpox, ricin, and yellow fever have been used against civilian populations throughout history. These deadly agents are concocted in laboratories every day in countries throughout the world. They can be easily smuggled across borders because they are small—a gram or less of many biotoxins could sicken or kill thousands of people. Some bioweapons can be cooked up by a competent team of chemistry students in a relatively inexpensive laboratory within the United States. Poisons such as ricin can be made in an average kitchen.

The World Health Organization states that smallpox poses "the most serious bioterrorist threat to the civilian population."[14] Smallpox is highly contagious and can be spread through face-to-face contact. The disease takes 12 to 14 days to cause symptoms such as fever, rash, and ulcers on the skin. If not treated, the symptoms lead to bleeding, vomiting, and death. Because of the extended period between recognition and infection, under what the NIC calls a "nightmare scenario,"[15] a terrorist smallpox attack could be well underway before authorities would understand what was happening. This might mean that hundreds of thousands of people could be infected with smallpox before steps could be taken to find the perpetrators or stop the developing epidemic. As scientist Tara O'Toole states: "There's . . . no theoretical limit on how many people you could kill if you mounted multiple attacks in many cities, over time."[16]

Such attacks could be executed by a terrorist wielding a handheld

> **Security experts believe that a deadly attack on U.S. soil within the next five to ten years is likely.**

aerosol on a train, bus, or airplane, or in a building. However, those wanting to cause the most damage might enact a scenario described by Alan Zelicoff, a leading expert on bioterrorism:

> One way would be for a van with a few pounds—we're not talking tons—of the organism . . . disseminating out of the back of the van through a spray nozzle. And the aerosol would be odorless and completely invisible. And because it's an aerosol . . . it behaves like the air, meaning it blows downwind just like the rest of the air does. And it doesn't settle. . . . [You're] talking about the ability to disseminate along, let's say, a long avenue somewhere and then . . . it would drift downwind for miles or tens of miles.[17]

A strike of this kind could threaten national security by causing mass panic, high casualties, and widespread economic disruption. However, some question whether terrorists could successfully execute a bioweapons attack. Writing in the *Washington Post*, John Mintz points out that there are numerous technical hurdles involved with manufacturing and disseminating bioweapons:

> **Hundreds of thousands of people could be infected with smallpox before steps could be taken to find the perpetrators or stop the developing epidemic.**

> Locating virulent anthrax specimens with which to brew an attack-size batch would be difficult given the medical community's caution about suspicious buyers. Smallpox could be next to impossible to obtain because it is thought to exist in only two secure sites, in Russia and in the United States. Creating aerosolized microbes also requires expertise in many arcane scientific disciplines, such as culturing and propagating germs that retain their virulence and "weaponizing" them so they float like a gas and enter the lungs easily.[18]

Whatever the case, between 2002 and 2006 the Department of Homeland Security spent $36 billion among 11 federal departments and agencies to address the threat of biological weapons. In 2007 the Bush administration proposed an additional $8 billion in bioweapons-related spending. The majority of this funding focuses on developing and purchasing medical countermeasures and protective equipment and enhancing medical surveillance and environmental detection of biological weapons agents. Only 2 percent of the funding is used to prevent the development, acquisition, and use of biological weapons by terrorists.

What Is the Threat from Nuclear Weapons?

As with bioweapons, the threat posed by nuclear weapons is a matter of heated debate. There is little doubt that al Qaeda would like to use nuclear weapons against Americans, as spokesmen for the group have made public pronouncements stating that their goal is to kill at least 4 million American men, women, and children in a coordinated attack. As Saudi cleric Nazer bin Hamd al-Fahd stated in a fatwa: "Weapons of mass destruction will kill the infidels on whom they fall, regardless of whether they are fighters, women or children. They will destroy and burn the land. The arguments for permissibility are many."[19]

> " The possible damage that could be caused by nuclear terrorism is so great that the government is spending billions of dollars to secure the borders, retrain weapons scientists in other countries, and lock up dangerous radioactive stockpiles. "

Experts believe the cleric was referring to a nuclear weapon because certain nuclear devices are small enough to fit into a delivery van. Such a weapon has the power to kill millions of people and cause trillions of dollars in economic damage. Former assistant secretary of defense Graham Allison explains the threat to national security posed by such a device:

> A single nuclear weapon . . . would have more explosive power than all the bombs dropped in all the wars in all of history. If such a bomb had gone off at the World Trade

Center . . . you would have seen not just the World Trade Center crumble but the whole southern tip of Manhattan disappear. You wouldn't have seen anything there; it would have vaporized.[20]

> "Observers believe that threats of terrorism are overblown and that few, if any, terrorists live in the United States."

How Likely Is a Nuclear Attack?

Those who believe that the nuclear threat is overblown point to enormous technical and logistical obstacles inherent in executing such an attack. Without sophisticated laboratories, expensive technology, and years of scientific experience, terrorists would have to either steal or buy an existing weapon. Even if this were possible, it is extremely difficult to set off a nuclear bomb since they have heat- and time-sensitive locking systems to prevent them from detonating accidentally. Still, the possible damage that could be caused by nuclear terrorism is so great that the government is spending billions of dollars to secure the borders, retrain weapons scientists in other countries, and lock up dangerous radioactive stockpiles.

"Almost No Terrorists Exist in the United States"

While security experts are in the business of imagining worst case scenarios, observers believe that threats of terrorism are overblown and that few, if any, terrorists live in the United States. For example, political science professor John Mueller says that politicians magnify the threats in order to gain votes by exploiting the public's fears. And the media sensationalizes possible terrorist threats to attract audiences. According to Mueller:

> [If] it is so easy to pull off an attack and if terrorists are so demonically competent, why have they not done it? Why have they not been sniping at people in shopping centers, collapsing tunnels, poisoning the food supply, cutting electrical lines, derailing trains, blowing up oil pipelines, causing massive traffic jams, or exploiting the countless other vulnerabilities that, according to security experts, could so easily be exploited? One reasonable explanation

is that almost no terrorists exist in the United States and few have the means or the inclination to strike from abroad. But this explanation is rarely offered.[21]

Despite Mueller's assessment, in a 2005 CNN poll 55 percent of Americans stated that terrorism and weapons of mass destruction were the top threats to U.S. national security. This opinion is undoubtedly driven by memory of the horrific attacks on 9/11. But while a terrorist attack may cause untold suffering for thousands of people, damage the national confidence, and create widespread fear and panic, it is unlikely that they can permanently harm the nation's physical integrity and territory or its economic relations with the rest of the world. If commentators like Mueller are correct, Americans should worry less. However, most government officials feel that it is their duty to protect the American people at any cost, and there is little doubt that they will continue to spend billions of dollars ensuring that terrorist attacks, no matter how remote, will not damage U.S. interests at home or abroad.

Primary Source Quotes*

How Serious a Threat Is Terrorism to National Security?

66 A terrorist cell may recruit in Southeast Asia, train in Central Asia, find funds in the Middle East and plan attacks in the U.S. or Europe. 99

—Hillary Clinton, "Challenges Facing the United States in the Global Security Environment," October 21, 2006. www.cfr.org.

Clinton is a U.S. senator from New York.

66 The terrorist threat is very real. It continues out there every day. . . . I think the extremists out there in al Qaeda are bound and determined to do everything they can to . . . kill Americans, including innocent civilians and women and children. . . . [You] can't negotiate with them. . . . You can't deter them. 99

—Richard Cheney, "Vice President Cheney Participates in Radio Interview," March 25, 2004. www.whitehouse.gov.

Cheney was elected vice president of the United States in 2000 and 2004.

Primary Source Quotes

66Foreign jihadists—individuals ready to fight any-where they believe Muslim lands are under attack by what they see as 'infidel invaders'—enjoy a growing sense of support from Muslims who are not necessar-ily supporters of terrorism.99

—Robert Hutchings, "Report of the National Intelligence Council's 2020 Project," National Intelligence Council, December 2004. www.dni.gov.

Hutchings is the director of the National Intelligence Council, a CIA think tank.

66Groups like al-Qaeda capitalize on the economic and political disenfranchisement to attract new recruits. Even historically local conflicts involving Muslim mi-norities or fundamentalist groups such as those in In-donesia, the Philippines and Thailand are generating new support for al-Qaeda and present new al-Qaeda-like threats.99

—Lowell E. Jacoby, "Current and Projected Security Threats to the United States," Defense Intelligence Agency, March 17, 2005. www.dia.mil.

Jacoby is a vice admiral in the U.S. Navy and director of the Defense Intelligence Agency.

66The current struggle [against terrorism] is reminis-cent of struggles in the last century against earlier totalitarian visions—fascism, communism, and Na-zism.99

—Stephen Hadley, "Remarks by National Security Advisor Stephen Hadley to the Council on Foreign Relations," White House, October 18, 2005. www.whitehouse.gov.

Hadley is national security adviser to George W. Bush.

&&America is now threatened less by conquering states than we are by failing ones. We are menaced less by fleets and armies than by catastrophic technologies in the hands of the embittered few.&&

—Joseph Nye, "The New Rome Meets the New Barbarians: American Power," *Economist,* March, 23, 2002, p. 3.

Nye is dean of the Harvard University Kennedy School of Government.

....

&&There is no elimination of risk in life, and anybody who promises every single person protection against every threat at every moment in every place in the country is making a false promise.&&

—Michael Chertoff, "Keynote Address by Secretary of Homeland Security Michael Chertoff to the 2006 Grants & Training National Conference," Department of Homeland Security, November 28, 2006. www.dhs.gov.

Chertoff is the secretary of the Department of Homeland Security.

....

&&[The] ports are the soft-underbelly of our nation's security. . . . [There is a] very real possibility that a weapon of mass destruction [may] be brought in a container and either detonated in a port near a busy metropolitan area or shipped in by rail or truck into the Heartland of our nation.&&

—Dianne Feinstein, "Statement of Senator Dianne Feinstein on Protecting America's Seaports from Terrorism," January 27, 2004. http://feinstein.senate.gov.

Feinstein is a U.S. senator from California.

....

66 The primary weapons of our enemies are not inanimate objects [such as bombs and anthrax spores], but rather the terrorists themselves. . . . Thus keeping the terrorists out or apprehending them after they get in is indispensable to victory [in the war on terrorism]. 99

—Mark Krikorian, "Keeping Terror Out: Immigration Policy and Asymmetric Warfare," Center for Immigration Studies, Spring 2000. www.cis.org.

Krikorian is the executive director of the Center for Immigration Studies.

66 With advances in the design of simplified nuclear weapons, terrorists will continue to seek to acquire fissile material in order to construct a nuclear weapon. 99

—Robert Hutchings, "Report of the National Intelligence Council's 2020 Project," National Intelligence Council, December 2004. www.dni.gov.

Hutchings is the director of the National Intelligence Council, a CIA think tank.

66 Acquiring the fissionable material to generate a nuclear explosion is the single most difficult step. But other daunting problems remain, including recruiting scientific experts in a broad array of disciplines, obtaining specialized industrial equipment, and avoiding the chemical and radiological hazards inherent in working with nuclear materials and high explosives. 99

—Council on Foreign Relations, "Terrorists' Nuclear Capabilities," January 2006. www.cfr.org.

The Council on Foreign Relations is an independent, nonpartisan foreign policy think tank founded in 1921.

How Serious a Threat Is Terrorism to National Security?

- When Timothy McVeigh bombed the Alfred P. Murrah Federal Building in Oklahoma City on April 19, 1995, killing **168**, it was the worst act of domestic terrorism in United States history.

- The September 11, 2001, terrorist attacks on the Pentagon and World Trade Center were planned for two years and cost less than **$500,000** to perform.

- In February 1998, Osama bin Laden published a **fatwa** declaring war on Jews and American Christians.

- The deadly ricin toxin can be extracted from the castor bean using average kitchen tools. Ricin is twice as deadly as cobra venom.

- The World Health Organization states that **smallpox** poses the most serious bioterrorist threat to civilians.

- The United States government spends about **$36 billion** a year to address the threats posed by biological weapons.

- If a 20 kiloton bomb (like the one dropped on Nagasaki, Japan) was detonated in New York city, **1.5 million** people would die immediately and an area 3.5 miles in diameter would be completely destroyed.

Where Will Terrorists Attack?

Security analysts believe that major cities in the United States are at risk for terrorist attack, but some cities are more vulnerable than others. As this graph indicates, on a scale of one to 10, New York City is overwhelmingly the most probable target, Chicago is a distant second, and Los Angeles is number six. The risk to other American cities is so low as to barely register on the graph.

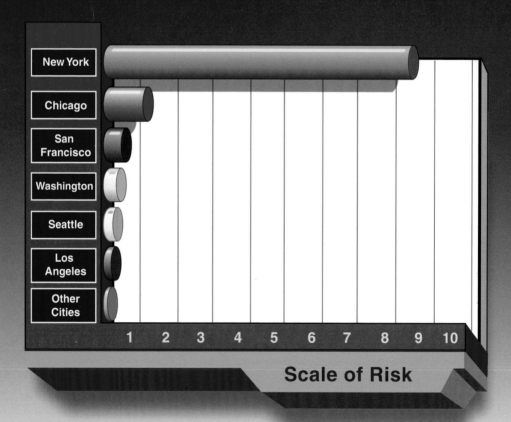

Scale of Risk

Source: Leslie Evans, "RAND Tries to Model Risks of Terrorist Attacks," UCLA International Institute, 2007. www.international.ucla.edu.

Dividing Up Dollars for National Security

Each dollar spent on national security is divided 3 ways. About 4 cents is spent on preventative measures such as spying on suspected terrorists. Homeland security receives about 7 cents to pay for security at airports and ports and to respond to terrorism emergencies. The bulk of the money, 89 cents, goes to the Department of Defense to maintain the military and fight wars.

One Dollar Spent on National Security

4 cents
Spending on preventative measures

7 cents
Spending on homeland security

89 cents
Military

Source: "National Security," National Priorities Project, December 21, 2006. http://nationalpriorities.org.

- Nuclear bombs have heat- and **time-sensitive** locking systems that prevent them from be detonated accidentally.

- More than **50 percent** of all Americans polled stated that terrorism and weapons of mass destruction are the top threats to United States national security.

Paying the Price for Bioterrorism Prevention

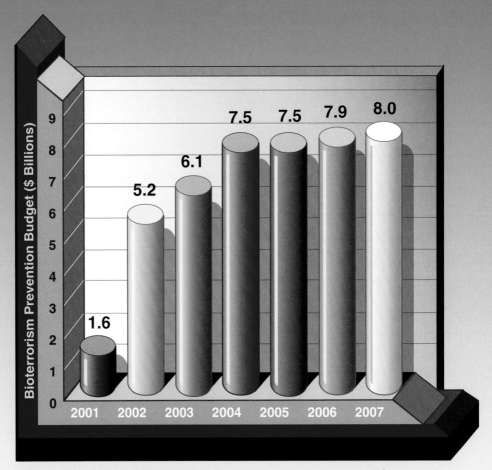

Bioterrorism Prevention Budget ($ Billions)

2001	2002	2003	2004	2005	2006	2007
1.6	5.2	6.1	7.5	7.5	7.9	8.0

Before the terrorist attacks of September 11, 2001, the United States only spent about $1.6 billion to research and prevent bioterrorism. Since that time, the budget for bioterrorism prevention and defense has climbed steadily to a high of $8 billion in 2007.

Source: "Federal Funding for Biological Weapons Prevention and Defense," Center for Arms Control and Non-Proliferation, 2006.

- On a global scale, the average person stands about a 1 in 80,000 chance of being killed by a terrorist, which is about the same as being killed by an asteroid.

Half of Americans Think Bush's Policy Made United States More Secure

Half of Americans think that Bush's policies on terrorism and national security have made the country a safer place to live, while more than a quarter feel the policies have made the United States less secure.

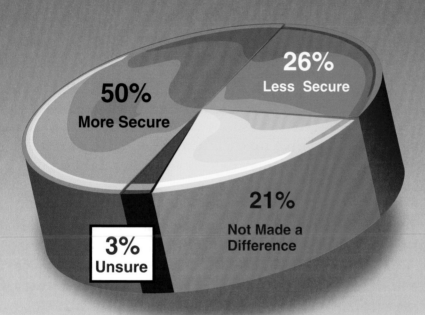

26%
Less Secure

50%
More Secure

21%
Not Made a Difference

3%
Unsure

"Have George Bush's policies on terrorism and national security made the country more secure, less secure, or have they made no difference one way or the other?"

Source: *Los Angeles Times* and Bloomberg Poll, December 2006.

How Do National Security Concerns Affect Privacy Rights?

66 Those who would give up essential Liberty, to purchase a little temporary Safety, deserve neither Liberty nor Safety. 99

—Benjamin Franklin, "The Quotable Franklin."

66 [To] those who scare peace-loving people with phantoms of lost liberty; my message is this: Your tactics only aid terrorists—for they erode our national unity and diminish our resolve. They give ammunition to America's enemies, and pause to America's friends. They encourage people of good will to remain silent in the face of evil. 99

—John Ashcroft, testimony of Attorney General John Ashcroft, Senate Committee on the Judiciary.

National security planners in the United States have long planned to fight enemies on foreign soil, protect American interests overseas, and engage distant nations in diplomatic negotiations. However, during the 20th century the focus on national security turned to domestic issues when it was feared that foreign agents could harm Americans by infiltrating government institutions or committing acts of violence at home.

The perceived threats to domestic security began around the time the

United States entered World War I in 1917. At that time some feared that European immigrants, Communists, and anarchists were trying to overthrow the American capitalist system. While the threat was largely exaggerated, the Bureau of Investigation, later the Federal Bureau of Investigation, began focusing its attention on the enforcement of domestic laws that protected national security. One such law, the Espionage Act of 1917, carried a 20-year sentence for anyone who passed on information that would interfere with the operation of the U.S. armed forces or promote the success of its enemies. Another law, the controversial Sedition Act of 1918, was passed to limit free speech by Americans who might "willfully utter, print, write, or publish any disloyal, profane, scurrilous, or abusive language"[22] about the government, flag, or armed forces.

> " The controversial Sedition Act of 1918 was passed to limit free speech by Americans who might 'willfully utter, print, write, or publish any disloyal, profane, scurrilous, or abusive language' about the government. "

Protecting the American Way of Life

The Sedition Act was used to convict nearly 900 people in 1919 and 1920, and their convictions were upheld by the Supreme Court. The act was subsequently repealed in 1921 as antithetical to the First Amendment guarantee of free speech. However, in the 1950s anti-Communist fears generated by the Cold War once again spurred government agencies to equate free speech and public assembly with threats to national security. Unlike the Sedition Act these new threats were not regulated by laws passed in Congress and reviewed by the courts. Instead they were dealt with in a top secret program, COINTELPRO, or Counter Intelligence Program, run by the FBI.

COINTELPRO was instituted in 1956 to disrupt the workings of the Communist Party USA, or in the words of the agency, "To stop the spread of communism, to stop the effectiveness of the Communist Party as a vehicle of Soviet intelligence, propaganda and agitation."[23] Explaining the rationale behind such activities, Cynthia A. Watson writes:

[The] United States defined national security not only as the defense of U.S. territorial integrity but our political path, our religious orientations, and other personal freedoms, all described in the phrase "the American way of life." Even though the Soviet Union had the military might to annihilate many urban areas of the United States, our main concern during the Cold War was actually being subjected to a political and ideological system that would suppress the exuberance and individual decision-making freedom of U.S. citizens.[24]

While most Americans agreed with such attitudes, the federal government used COINTELPRO for its own political purposes. In the name of protecting national security on the domestic front, the FBI went after individuals who were exercising their First Amendment rights to free speech and assembly in order to protest racial segregation and war in Vietnam. Techniques used by the government often violated the Fourth Amendment safeguards against unreasonable searches and included opening mail, breaking into offices, and tapping phones without search warrants. FBI agents also illegally worked to get targets fired from their jobs, prevented them from giving speeches, and subjected them to exhaustive tax audits for spurious reasons.

In addition to the FBI, the CIA conducted similar activities under a program called Operation Chaos, which involved spying on people who opposed the war in Vietnam or were purported black nationalists. Operation Chaos was made possible by the FBI, which shared tens of thousands of reports on the American peace movement with the CIA every year. This occurred despite laws that prohibit the CIA from engaging in law enforcement or security functions involving Americans.

> " In the name of protecting national security . . . the FBI went after individuals who were exercising their First Amendment rights to free speech and assembly in order to protest racial segregation and war in Vietnam. "

The Foreign Intelligence Surveillance Act

In the mid-1970s, a Senate committee exposed the abuses of Operation Chaos and COINTELPRO, which prompted Congress to pass the Foreign Intelligence Surveillance Act (FISA) of 1978. When creating FISA, Congress recognized the legitimate function of intelligence agencies to investigate individuals in the interest of national security. However, FISA also attempted to balance privacy rights with the government's need to protect Americans from unlawful conduct by federal agents.

Under FISA, a special secret court, the Foreign Intelligence Surveillance Court (FISC), is overseen by seven federal district court judges from around the country. Intelligence agencies who wish to conduct electronic eavesdropping or wiretapping have to obtain special warrants from the court. All decisions of the FISA are subject to review by the House Permanent Select Committee on Intelligence and the Senate Select Committee on Intelligence.

> " When creating [the Foreign Intelligence Surveillance Act], Congress recognized the legitimate function of intelligence agencies to investigate individuals in the interest of national security. "

Targets of FISA are generally meant to be foreign powers or agents of foreign powers, but the law allows an investigation of a U.S. citizen or permanent resident alien who "knowingly engages in activities in preparation for sabotage or international terrorism on behalf of a foreign power."[25]

Over the years, FISA has generally been accepted as a means for protecting both privacy rights and government interests, as Marion E. Bowman, deputy general counsel for the FBI, tells Congress: "FISA has proved its worth on countless occasions in preventing the occurrence or the continuation of harm to the national security. It has been a very effective tool and time has proved that this cooperative effort of the three branches of government can serve to protect the public without eroding civil liberties."[26]

The USA Patriot Act

FISA became much more controversial after the September 11, 2001, terrorist attacks. On October 26, 2001, Congress passed an all-encompassing antiterrorism bill, the USA PATRIOT Act, which made significant changes in FISA. For example, when FISA was first passed, it limited intelligence sharing between the CIA, NSA, and FBI so that information gathered for intelligence purposes could not be used in criminal investigations. However, the Patriot Act eliminated this "wall," prompting fears that intelligence gathered through FISA could be used by law enforcement agencies to harass or intimidate American citizens exercising their free speech rights.

FISA was also amended to expand the use of pen registers and trap and trace devices, surveillance tools that capture phone numbers and identify incoming calls. These spy devices can now be used in any FISA investigation without having to establish that the target is a foreigner or an agent of a foreign power. The changes in the law prompted criticism from the Electronic Freedom Foundation, a privacy rights organization: "FISA powers are broad and vague, and . . . FISA power extends well beyond spies and terrorists. It can be used in connection with ordinary criminal investigations involving United States citizens who live in this country."[27]

While these technical changes have generated little controversy among the general public, other aspects of the Patriot Act contain provisions that civil libertarians believe are unconstitutional. For example, Section 215 allows authorities to search personal records of anyone without proof that a crime has been committed. Section 411 makes it a crime to associate with terrorists even if a person is unaware that he or she is doing so.

> **Attorney General Alberto Gonzales stated that Congress granted the president unlimited powers when it passed a provision . . . called the Authorization for Use of Military Force.**

The Patriot Act was originally written with "sunset" provisions to nullify 14 of the 16 sections in five years. However, in March 2006 most provisions were made a permanent part of the law. The controversial

Section 215 is set to expire in 2010. When the bill was reauthorized in 2006, it was reported that the Patriot Act was used in at least 30,000 national security investigations every year. President Bush stated that the law helped convict 200 people. However, according to Justice Department statistics, only one of those people was guilty of crimes relating to terrorism or national security. The rest were involved with Colombian drug cartels, Rwandan war crimes, or other issues. According to the *Washington Post,* "The results from the Justice Department . . . raise the possibility that the presence of al Qaeda operatives and sympathizers within the United States is either limited or largely undetected."[28]

Wiretapping Americans

The government has instituted other investigations that evaded provisions of the original FISA law. In December 2005 the *New York Times* reported that the president authorized the NSA to wiretap hundreds of thousands of American citizens without warrants from FISC. However, in explaining the action, Attorney General Alberto Gonzales stated that Congress granted the president unlimited powers when it passed a provision a week after 9/11 called the Authorization for Use of Military Force: "In the authorization to use military force Congress has told the president of the United States, you may engage in all the activities that are fundamentally incidental to waging war."[29]

> " The president authorized the NSA to wiretap hundreds of thousands of American citizens without warrants. "

Civil libertarians disagreed with the assessment and stated that by authorizing the program, the president himself posed a threat to national security. Former vice president Al Gore commented on the issue in a speech at Washington, D.C.'s Constitutional Hall: "What we do know about this pervasive wiretapping virtually compels the conclusion that the President of the United States has been breaking the law repeatedly and persistently. A president who breaks the law is a threat to the very structure of our government."[30]

While Gore and others argue over the legality of the NSA wiretaps, national security experts point out that, like the Patriot Act, the eavesdropping has yielded few tangible results. In February 2006 the *Washington Post* reported:

> Intelligence officers who eavesdropped on thousands of Americans . . . under authority from President Bush have dismissed nearly all of them as potential suspects after hearing nothing pertinent to a terrorist threat. . . . Fewer than 10 U.S. citizens or residents a year, according to an authoritative account, have aroused enough suspicion during warrantless eavesdropping to justify [further investigation]."[31]

Investigating Private Records

The NSA is not the only government agency investigating millions of Americans in the name of national security. After 9/11 the government authorized dozens of other agencies to focus on electronic intelligence concerning national security. These agencies retain military and civilian analysts who use computers to "mine" data; that is, search through trillions of private electronic records such as credit card statements, financial transactions, Internet searches, airline bookings, medical records, and immigration records. The analysts are looking for patterns of behavior that might indicate terrorist activities. An example was discovered by the FBI when the agency combed through consumer data bases and learned that 1 of the hijackers had been in the country less than 2 years. Suspiciously, during that short period, he had used 30 different credit cards and had run up $250,000 in debt. It was also learned that ringleader Mohammad Atta had been in the country two years but had moved 12 times and used several different names. While this information was not discovered until after the 9/11 attacks, the patterns of behavior have pro-

> " The data-mining process produces false alarms that force government agents to investigate innocent citizens simply because of unusual patterns detected by the software. "

vided insight into the inner workings of terrorist groups.

Some security experts doubt that such information could be detected before an attack, given the billions of records generated every day. Many times the data-mining process produces false alarms that force government agents to investigate innocent citizens simply because of unusual patterns detected by the software. Others perceive data mining as an invasion of privacy rights. Whatever the case, in May 2006 the Government Accountability Office reported that 52 federal agencies were operating nearly 200 data mining programs.

Americans and the Constitution

As long as there are threats to the United States, the debate over national security and privacy rights will continue. As Massachusetts senator Edward Kennedy says: "The president has the constitutional obligation to protect and defend the American people. That is obvious—but he also took an oath of office, to 'preserve, protect and defend the Constitution of the United States.'"[32] The job of defending both Americans and the Constitution remains extremely difficult. And it will remain so as long as few people are willing to sacrifice either personal privacy or the national security of the United States.

How Do National Security Concerns Affect Privacy Rights?

❝The right of the people to be secure in their persons, houses, papers, and effects, against unreasonable searches and seizures, shall not be violated, and no warrants shall issue, but upon probable cause, supported by oath or affirmation, and particularly describing the place to be searched, and the persons or things to be seized.❞

—U.S. Constitution, Fourth Amendment. http://usinfo.state.gov.

The Fourth Amendment is part of the Bill of Rights, which consists of the first 10 amendments to the U.S. Constitution.

❝[The Patriot Act] is essential not only to pursuing and punishing terrorists, but also preventing more atrocities in the hands of the evil ones. This government will enforce this law with all the urgency of a nation at war.... [We are] united in our resolve to fight and stop and punish those who would do harm to the American people.❞

—George W. Bush, "President Signs Anti-Terrorism Bill," White House, October 26, 2001. www.whitehouse.gov.

Bush is the forty-third president of the United States.

Bracketed quotes indicate conflicting positions.

* Editor's Note: While the definition of a primary source can be narrowly or broadly defined, for the purposes of Compact Research, a primary source consists of: 1) results of original research presented by an organization or researcher; 2) eyewitness accounts of events, personal experience, or work experience; 3) first-person editorials offering pundits' opinions; 4) government officials presenting political plans and/or policies; 5) representatives of organizations presenting testimony or policy.

Primary Source Quotes

"If you are angry . . . because our government officials did not protect us on 9/11, why on earth would you give the same government more power and access to your life without at least questioning it?"

—David Hunt, *They Just Don't Get It: How Washington Is Still Compromising Your Safety—and What You Can Do About It.* New York: Crown Forum, 2005, p. 168.

Hunt is a retired U.S. Army colonel and counterterrorism and intelligence expert.

....

"[Not] one of the civil liberties groups has cited one instance of abuse of our constitutional rights, one decision by any court that any part of the Patriot Act was unconstitutional or one shred of evidence to contradict the fact that these tools protect what is perhaps our most important civil liberty: the freedom from future terrorist attacks."

—Orrin Hatch, "In Defense of the Patriot Act," *Frontpage Magazine*, May 14, 2003. http://frontpagemag.com.

Hatch is a U.S. senator from Utah.

....

"In its zeal to expand the power of the President, the Bush administration's actions have threatened the fabric of the Constitution. . . . It would be one thing if the President's actions to expand Presidential power reflected sound judgment and wisdom. But again and again, the President's overreaching in the name of security has been profoundly misguided, and has undermined support for the war against al-Qaida at home and abroad."

—Joseph Biden, "Extension of the USA Patriot Act," *Congressional Record*, December 21, 2005. www.fas.org.

Biden is a U.S. senator from Delaware.

....

66 The terrorist surveillance program was highly classified, and information about it was improperly given to the news media. As the Attorney General pointed out . . . it's easy to imagine America's enemies shaking their heads in amazement that anyone would disclose this information, thereby giving notice to those enemies, damaging national security, and putting our citizens at risk. 99

—Richard Cheney, "Remarks by the Vice President on the 2006 Agenda," White House, February 9, 2006. www.whitehouse.gov.

Cheney is the forty-sixth vice president of the United States.

66 [The NSA] strictly follows laws and regulations designed to preserve every American's privacy rights under the Fourth Amendment to the United States Constitution. 99

—National Security Agency, "Signals Intelligence," 2006. www.nsa.gov.

The National Security Agency is the government intelligence agency in charge of monitoring electronic communications.

66 The president is the commander in chief of the military. That doesn't give him the power to spy on civilians at home without any judicial oversight whatsoever, without ever revealing those activities to even well-established courts that review these matters in secrecy. 99

—Edward Kennedy, "On Wiretapping Bush Isn't Listening to the Constitution," *Boston Globe*, December 22, 2005. www.boston.com.

Kennedy is a U.S. senator from Massachusetts.

66In a time of war, the President has tried to act in a way that meets the needs and obligations of a Commander-in-Chief against a dispersed and highly-unique kind of enemy.99

—Tony Snow, "Press Briefing by Tony Snow," White House, June 29, 2006. www.whitehouse.gov.

Snow is a broadcaster, newspaper columnist, and press secretary for George W. Bush.

66Many of the relevant bits [of information indicating a pending terrorist attack] may be in the e-mails, phone conversations or banking records of U.S. citizens, some innocent, some not so innocent. The government is entitled to those data, but just for the limited purpose of protecting national security.99

—Richard A. Posner, "Our Domestic Intelligence Crisis," *Washington Post*, December 21, 2005. www.washingtonpost.com.

Posner is a judge on the U.S. Court of Appeals for the Seventh Circuit.

66[If] this Nation is to remain true to the ideals symbolized by its flag, it must not wield the tools of tyrants even to resist an assault by the forces of tyranny.99

—John Paul Stevens, "Stevens, J. Dissenting, *Rumsfeld v. Padilla*" Supreme Court of the United States, October 2003. www.law.duke.edu.

Stevens has been a member of the U.S. Supreme Court since 1975.

66All data mining systems fail in two different ways: false positives and false negatives. A false positive is when the system identifies a terrorist plot that really isn't one. A false negative is when the system misses an actual terrorist plot.99

—Bruce Schneier, "Data Mining for Terrorists," *Schneier on Security*, March 9, 2006. www.schneier.com.

Schneier is an author and expert in security technology.

Facts and Illustrations

How Do National Security Concerns Affect Privacy Rights?

- The Foreign Intelligence Surveillance Act regulates intelligence agencies that are investigating **foreign agents** suspected of terrorism or American citizens who might be aiding them.

- The Foreign Intelligence Surveillance Court issues warrants to federal agencies wishing to conduct electronic **eavesdropping** or wiretapping.

- The **USA PATRIOT Act** was signed by President George W. Bush on October 26, 2001. The law strengthened criminal penalties against terrorists, enhanced government powers to conduct surveillance against suspects, and allowed government agencies broad new powers to monitor the activities of Americans.

- Section 215 of the Patriot Act allows authorities to search **personal records** of innocent citizens, including bank statements, medical files, and records of videos rented and books checked out of the library.

- Most provisions of the Patriot Act that were set to expire five years after their passage were made a permanent part of federal law on **March 9, 2006**.

- Using provisions in the Patriot Act, the FBI has investigated about **30,000** people a year since 2002.

Warrants for Wiretapping

When intelligence authorities want to wiretap a suspect's telephone, they must determine if the parties involved are United States citizens. As this graph shows, if the suspects are citizens, a warrant under the Foreign Intellligence Surveillance Act (FISA) must be obtained. However, if the suspects are foreigners, or if they are communicating in a foreign country, a FISA warrant is not necessary.

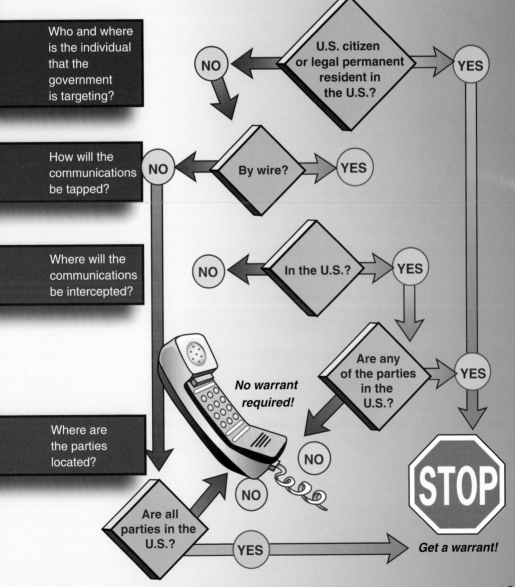

Source: "FISA Wiretapping Diagram," Bill of Rights Defense Committee, 2007. www.bordc.org.

Public Opinion on the Patriot Act

When *USA Today*/CNN pollsters asked Americans in 2004 about the Patriot Act, 43 percent of those polled responded that the law was balanced between restricting civil liberties and fighting terrorism. Twenty-six percent said it went too far.

Do you think the Patriot Act goes too far, is about right, or does not go far enough in restricting people's civil liberties in order to fight terrorism?"

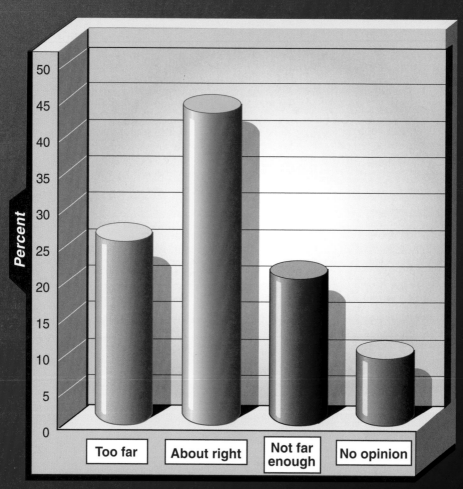

Source: "U.S. Public Opinion on Patriot Act," Bill of Rights Defense Committee, 2007. www.bordc.org.

The NSA Surveillance Network

The National Security Agency (NSA) located in Washington, D.C., has an extensive web of satellite, Internet, and telephone listening posts to conduct surveillance on communications throughout the world. This map shows how and where the NSA connects into voice and data communications.

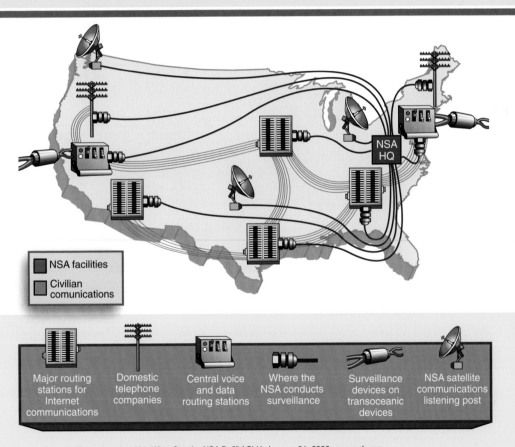

NSA facilities

Civilian comunications

Major routing stations for Internet communications

Domestic telephone companies

Central voice and data routing stations

Where the NSA conducts surveillance

Surveillance devices on transoceanic devices

NSA satellite communications listening post

Source: "Eavesdropping 101: What Can the NSA Do?" ACLU, January 31, 2006. www.aclu.org.

- The National Security Agency monitors, without search warrants, telephone calls made by private citizens within the United States.

- The NSA eavesdropping program has yielded less than **10 suspects**, none of whom were convicted of terrorist offenses.

Public Opinion on Wiretapping

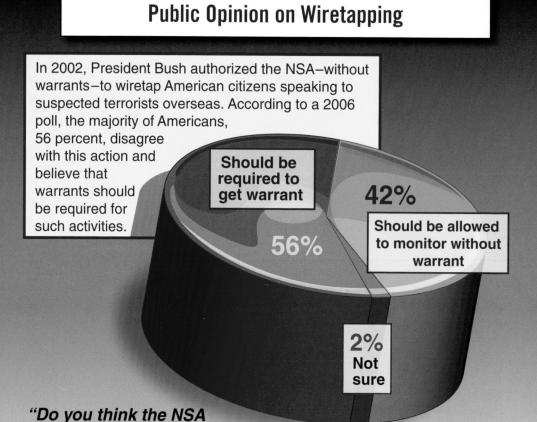

In 2002, President Bush authorized the NSA—without warrants—to wiretap American citizens speaking to suspected terrorists overseas. According to a 2006 poll, the majority of Americans, 56 percent, disagree with this action and believe that warrants should be required for such activities.

Should be required to get warrant

56%

42%

Should be allowed to monitor without warrant

2% Not sure

"Do you think the NSA should be required to obtain a warrant to monitor communications between American citizens and suspected terrorists overseas?"

Source: Bob Egelko, "Spy Powers," *San Francisco Chronicle*, January 8, 2006. www.sfgate.com.

- The Government Accountability Office reports that 52 federal agencies are operating nearly **200** data-mining programs.

- Data mining often produces **false alarms** that force government agents to investigate innocent citizens simply because of unusual patterns detected by data-mining software.

How Does U.S. Foreign Policy Affect National Security?

>❝We will defend the peace by fighting terrorists and tyrants. We will preserve the peace by building good relations among the great powers. We will extend the peace by encouraging free and open societies on every continent.❞
>
> —George W. Bush, "The National Security Strategy of the United States of America."

>❝The Bush Doctrine poses a greater danger to the United States than do the perils it supposedly guards against.❞
>
> —Andrew J. Bacevich, "Rescinding the Bush Doctrine."

Foreign policy is a major component of U.S. national security and has been ever since Benjamin Franklin negotiated the Treaty of Paris in 1783 to end the Revolutionary War. In the centuries that followed, diplomats, negotiators, scholars, and lawyers have formulated foreign policy to protect the economic interests, ideological goals, and national security of the United States.

In the second half of the 20th century, foreign policy experts in the State Department were largely concerned with the Soviet Union. They wanted to prevent the Soviets from taking control of smaller nations and installing

Communist governments in Western Europe, Asia, Africa, South America, and the Caribbean. To do so, some government and military leaders wanted to use the military to force the Soviets out of Eastern Europe and push them back to their pre–World War II borders. Since the USSR possessed nuclear weapons and commanded a million-man army, this policy was deemed impractical. Instead, the government engaged in a policy of containment based on the theories of political scientist, historian, and diplomat George Kennan who formulated the strategy in 1947.

Kennan, known as the "father of containment," understood that the Soviets wanted to expand their sphere of influence throughout the world. He believed, however, it would be a mistake to attack the USSR unless it attacked the United States first. Instead, the United States should engage in tactics known as the carrot and stick, or reward and punishment. First, the United States should promote the superiority of the American system and win the "hearts and minds" of citizens throughout the world by showing how capitalism can improve their standard of living. Those who ignored such appeals and drifted toward communism would face the stick, punishment in the form of economic sanctions and diplomatic isolation. Kennan also believed that the United States should pit its adversaries against one another; for example, favoring China over the USSR to create distrust between those two nations.

> Kennan ... believed that the Soviet Union would eventually collapse because its military was overextended in Eastern Europe, and the economic system of communism was impossible to sustain.

Kennan stated that U.S. policy should be built on "long-term, patient but firm and vigilant containment of Russian expansive tendencies."[33] He believed that the Soviet Union would eventually collapse because its military was overextended in Eastern Europe, and the economic system of communism was impossible to sustain.

Kennan's theories were also backed by military power under a foreign policy known as the Truman Doctrine, after President Harry Truman. The Truman Doctrine stated that the United States would provide economic and military aid to any nation that resisted the Soviet Union. In Truman's words, it became "the policy of the United States to support free peoples who are resisting attempted subjugation by armed minorities or by outside pressures."[34] During the Cold War the Truman Doctrine was first used when the United States sent $400 million to Greece to help it resist takeover by several thousand Communist rebels. In the years that followed, the Truman Doctrine was often implemented by the CIA, which provided money and military expertise to nations fending off Communist insurgents. In several cases, such as Korea and Vietnam, the United States provided troops to fight Communist-backed forces.

Forging Alliances in the United Nations

While engaging in proxy wars in nations like Vietnam, the United States forged diplomatic alliances with foreign nations—including the Soviet Union—when necessary. The center of this coalition building was the United Nations (UN), founded in 1945 with the stated purpose of helping nations avoid the "scourge of war."[35] The UN Charter established several councils, such as the Economic and Social Council and the International Court of Justice, to help solve international problems. It also established a military staff to oversee international peacekeeping forces. The UN Security Council is made up of five permanent members, the United States, Great Britain, the Soviet Union, France, and China Each nation had veto power over any UN peacekeeping action.

> " The United States forged diplomatic alliances with foreign nations—including the Soviet Union—when necessary. "

The UN's first test of unity came in 1950 when Communist North Korea invaded South Korea. Through the UN, the United States assembled an international force of 19 nations and obtained a UN endorsement to fight North Korea. Describing this event, Craig R. Eisendrath and Melvin A. Goodman write in *Bush League Diplomacy*, "[The] Korean War was an important reminder that diplomacy was of critical importance to international security, that collective security was essential, and that the threat of confrontation required new efforts to prevent the scourge of war."[36]

The UN also protected U.S. interests concerning a broad range of economic, military, and social issues, forging agreements on arms control, international aviation, telecommunications, tariffs, trade, world health, and refugees. As Eisendrath and Goodman write, "Diplomacy was not just another option but the primary means by which the United States worked with other states to create [national] security."[37]

The Bush Doctrine

Critics of the United Nations believed that its massive bureaucracy prevented it from acting in a decisive manner. In addition, the Security Council was often divided between the United States on one side and China and the Soviets on the other. Since all members could wield veto power, oftentimes nothing could be agreed upon. Long a target of conservatives, Republicans in Congress began pulling away from the UN in the 1980s and 1990s, refusing to pay dues owed to the organization by the United States, which totaled hundreds of millions of dollars. The anti-UN trend continued in the twenty-first century as the United States pursued an international policy based on unilateralism; that is, a foreign policy with little regard for the views of other nations.

> " **Under the Bush Doctrine the United States maintains the right to military preemption.** "

Unilateralism is the basis for what is known as the Bush Doctrine, named for President George W. Bush. This foreign policy, formulated in 2002, has several key points that depart from the containment policies that characterized the Cold War. Under the Bush Doctrine the United States maintains the right to military preemption. That is, instead of acting in self-defense after enemies attack, the United States reserves the right to wage preemptive war unilaterally against nations that are perceived as emerging threats. According to the doctrine, published under the title "The National Security Strategy of the United States of America," the government will defend

the United States, the American people, and our interests at home and abroad by identifying and destroying the threat before it reaches our borders. While the United

States will constantly strive to enlist the support of the international community, we will not hesitate to act alone, if necessary, to exercise our right of self-defense by acting preemptively against [enemies] to prevent them from doing harm against our people and our country.[38]

> **The United States provides money and military support to repressive antidemocratic leaders in Egypt, Saudi Arabia, and elsewhere.**

Another facet of the Bush Doctrine favors strength beyond challenge, meaning that the United States will maintain the largest military force in the world in order to keep its sole superpower status. Finally, the Bush Doctrine offers to extend democracy, liberty, and security to all regions of the world. In the words of the president: "America has no empire to extend or utopia to establish. We wish for others only what we wish for ourselves—safety from violence, the rewards of liberty, and the hope for a better life."[39]

The key points of the Bush Doctrine have been supported by conservatives for decades. However, in the aftermath of the 9/11 terrorist attacks the policies gained wider support, as Ian Shapiro writes in the *Los Angeles Times*: "If Al Qaeda is attacking and nuclear terrorists are roaming the globe and rogue governments are providing them with weapons . . . only radical measures—preemptive war and forcible regime change—can protect us."[40]

The Bush Doctrine in Iraq

Critics of the Bush Doctrine say that the concept of preemptive war violates the UN Charter to which the United States is a signatory. For example, Article 2 of the charter states, "All Members shall settle their international disputes by peaceful means in such a manner that international peace and security, and justice, are not endangered."[41]

Another criticism of the Bush Doctrine concerns the stated purpose of supporting democracy in the Middle East. In reality, the United States provides money and military support to repressive antidemocratic leaders in Egypt, Saudi Arabia, and elsewhere. And in several nations, when free and fair elections are held, the United States does not support democracy when anti-American political parties win. This was seen in the elections in Palestine in 2006 when the terrorist group Hamas swept to victory, causing the Bush administration to cut off aid to the new government and to refuse to speak to its leaders. This prompted Hamas supporter Nawaf Musawi to say: "It's funny . . . how the United States is so strongly in favor of democracy but all its friends in the region are despotic regimes. Those regimes remain in power with American support. We also rely on support, but our support is . . . from our people."[42]

A Nuclear Iran

Beyond democratic elections, the Bush Doctrine has also generated controversy when applied to foreign policy hot spots throughout the world. For example, Iran has been developing a nuclear program since the mid-1990s. Iranian leaders claim that the program has been put in place to develop nuclear power plants for electricity, but U.S. intelligence sources believe Iran is building nuclear bombs, which will be completed between 2012 and 2015. If true, Iran's nuclear program poses several problems for the United States and its allies. As a country ruled by conservative Muslim leaders, Iran is a sworn enemy of Israel and the United States and is dedicated to the destruction of both nations. As Iranian President Mahmoud Ahmadinejad stated in 2006, "Israel must be wiped off the map. . . . And God willing, with the force of God behind it, we shall soon experience a world without the United States and Zionism."[43] If Iran were to launch a nuclear attack against Israel, that nation, along with the United States, would respond with their own nuclear weapons. This would create a catastrophe in the Middle East that would be nearly impossible to measure, killing millions of people and creating an environmental disaster as clouds of highly toxic radioactive dust lofted high into the

> "When free and fair elections are held, the United States does not support democracy when anti-American political parties win."

atmosphere and encircled the globe for years.

Until 2007 the United States refused to negotiate with Iran on the grounds that Iran supports terrorist organizations such as al Qaeda. According to the Bush Doctrine, the United States will make no concessions to terrorists or nations that support them. And as the National Security Strategy makes clear:

> [The United States] may face no greater challenge from a single country than from Iran. The Iranian regime sponsors terrorism; threatens Israel; seeks to thwart Middle East peace; disrupts democracy in Iraq; and denies the aspirations of its people for freedom. [The] first duty of the United States Government remains what it always has been: to protect the American people and American interests. It is an enduring American principle that this duty obligates the government to anticipate and counter threats, using all elements of national power, before the threats can do grave damage.[44]

> **The United States refused to negotiate with Iran on the grounds that Iran supports terrorist organizations such as al Qaeda.**

In 2007 administration critics feared that such language was being used to justify a unilateral, preemptive military strike on Iran's nuclear facilities. However, the Bush administration continued to deny such scenarios, and the United States offered to open limited diplomatic relations with Iran if that nation agreed to stop enriching uranium, which could be used to construct a nuclear weapon.

Whatever the future may hold for the Middle East, the Bush Doctrine has shown that a president may strike out on a controversial course of action if national security is threatened. Whether the United States continues to follow the foreign policy dictates laid out by Bush after his term in office expires will be determined by who is elected president in 2008. Until that time, the State Department, the Department of Defense, and the intelligence services will uphold a policy of unilateralism and preemptive war.

Primary Source Quotes*

How Does U.S. Foreign Policy Affect National Security?

"[It] is hard to think of America and the world today without the profound effect that [George] Kennan had on averting a hot and possibly nuclear war instead of a half-century of cold war, that ended as he predicted it would."

—Daniel Schorr, "Kennan's Profound Global Effect," *Christian Science Monitor*, March 21, 2005. www.csmonitor.com.

Schorr is the senior news analyst at National Public Radio.

"This whole tendency to see ourselves as the center of political enlightenment and as teachers to a great part of the rest of the world strikes me as unthought-through, vainglorious, and undesirable. If you think that our life here at home has meritorious aspects . . . the best way to recommend them is . . . not by preaching at others but by the force of example."

—George F. Kennan, "George F. Kennan on the Web," Russil Wvong, March 22, 2005. www.geocities.com.

Kennan is the political scientist, historian, and diplomat who formulated the U.S. Cold War containment strategy in 1947.

Bracketed quotes indicate conflicting positions.

* Editor's Note: While the definition of a primary source can be narrowly or broadly defined, for the purposes of Compact Research, a primary source consists of: 1) results of original research presented by an organization or researcher; 2) eyewitness accounts of events, personal experience, or work experience; 3) first-person editorials offering pundits' opinions; 4) government officials presenting political plans and/or policies; 5) representatives of organizations presenting testimony or policy.

❝The United Nations . . . shall not realize [its] objectives . . . unless we are willing to help free peoples to maintain their free institutions and their national integrity against aggressive movements that seek to impose upon them totalitarian regimes.❞

—Harry S. Truman, "The Truman Doctrine," Yale Law School, 1997. www.yale.edu.

Truman was the thirty-third president of the United States from 1945 to 1953.

❝The United States national security strategy will be based on a distinctly American internationalism that reflects the union of our values and our national interests. . . . Our goals on the path to progress are clear: political and economic freedom, peaceful relations with other states, and respect for human dignity.❞

—George W. Bush, "The National Security Strategy of the United States of America," White House, September 20, 2002. www.whitehouse.gov.

Bush is the forty-third president of the United States.

❝[The Bush Doctrine] repudiates the core idea of the United Nations Charter, which prohibits any use of international force that is not undertaken in self-defense after the occurrence of an armed attack across an international boundary.❞

—Richard Falk, "The New Bush Doctrine," *Nation*, June 27, 2002. www.thenation.com.

Falk is professor of international law and practice at the University of California at Santa Barbara.

66 America's universal political principles and unprecedented global power and influence make the Bush Doctrine a whole greater than the sum of its parts; it is likely to remain the basis for U.S. security strategy for decades to come. 99

—Thomas Donnelly, "The Underpinnings of the Bush Doctrine," American Enterprise Institute, January 31, 2003. www.aei.org.

Donnelly is a defense and security policy analyst and former editor of *Armed Forces Journal*, *Army Times*, and *Defense News*.

66 Since the Bush Doctrine was formulated, the U.S. military has become bogged down in Iraq, the federal budget has gone from massive surplus to massive deficit, international support and respect for America have fallen to new depths, and the President's domestic support—especially for the war in Iraq—has fallen considerably. 99

—Philip H. Gordon, "The Bush Doctrine," Brookings Institution, March 8, 2007. www.brookings.edu.

Gordon is a senior fellow for U.S. foreign policy at the Brookings Institution, a private organization devoted to analyzing public policy issues at the national level.

66 In pursuing its revolutionary idea to forcibly democratize a region in order to fight Islamic extremism, the Bush administration has unwittingly pushed some countries to elect governments that are more sympathetic to the Islamic extremist movement than with the United States. 99

—James Salterio, "Bush Doctrine Dead (Like It Ever Stood a Chance)," *Current U.S. and World News*, July 13, 2006. http://worldandpolitics.blogspot.com.

Salterio is a blogger for the *Current U.S. and World News* Web site.

> **"Iran is likely continuing nuclear weapon–related endeavors in an effort to become the dominant regional power and deter what it perceives as the potential for US or Israeli attack."**

—Lowell E. Jacoby, "Current and Projected Security Threats to the United States," Defense Intelligence Agency, March 17, 2005. www.dia.mil.

Jacoby is a vice admiral in the U.S. Navy and director of the Defense Intelligence Agency.

> **"The Bush administration's rhetorical justifications for invading Iraq were to . . . inspire the "democratization" of the Middle East. But continued Bush administration support for equally brutal, but "friendly," regimes reveals the hypocrisy of those justifications and the emptiness of the administration's goal of spreading democracy."**

—Ivan Eland, "With Friends Like These, U.S. Enemies Don't Seem as Bad," Independent Institute, January 7, 2004. www.independent.org.

Eland is director of the Center on Peace & Liberty at the Independent Institute and assistant editor of the *Independent Review*.

> **"There have been three national elections in Iraq, there's a democracy established there, a constitution, a new democratically elected government, Saddam has been brought to justice and executed . . . and the world is better off for it."**

—Richard Cheney, "Interview of the Vice President by Wolf Blitzer, CNN 'Situation Room,'" White House, January 24, 2007. www.whitehouse.gov.

Cheney is the forty-sixth vice president of the United States.

“An Iran armed with the nuclear bomb would surely persuade countries like Saudi Arabia, Egypt and Jordan, nervous of Iran's aggressiveness, to contemplate arming themselves with nuclear weapons, thus turning the Middle East into a region of instability.”

—John Hughes, "What Is Real Threat of a Nuclear North Korea?" *Deseret Morning News*, October 18, 2006. www.deseretnews.com.

Hughes is the editor and CEO of the *Deseret Morning News* in Salt Lake City.

Facts and Illustrations

How Does U.S. Foreign Policy Affect National Security?

- During the **Cold War**, the United States practiced a policy of containment with the Soviet Union, promoting the superiority of the American system worldwide while punishing nations with economic sanctions and diplomatic isolation if they supported communism.

- **Article 2** of the United Nations Charter states that "All Members shall settle their international disputes by peaceful means in such a manner that international peace and security, and justice, are not endangered."

- In 1950 the United States worked with the United Nations to assemble an international force of **19 nations** to fight the North Korean invasion of South Korea.

- President George W. Bush unveiled the **Bush Doctrine** in "The National Security Strategy of the United States of America" on September 20, 2002.

- The Bush Doctrine asserts that the United States has the right to unilaterally engage in **preemptive war** if it is in the interest of national security.

- The United States has the world's largest military budget and in 2007 the **$522 billion** allocated to the Defense Department was equal to about half of all military spending in the world.

How the U.S. Contained the Soviet Union

This 1959 map of the world demonstrates George Kennan's containment theory concerning the Soviet Union. The arrows indicate how the United States put pressure on the Soviets by developing friendly economic, political, and diplomatic relations with the Asian nations to the east, India and the Middle East to the south, and Europe to the west. In this manner the expansionist tendencies of the Soviet Union were kept in check by allies whose interests coincided with those of the United States.

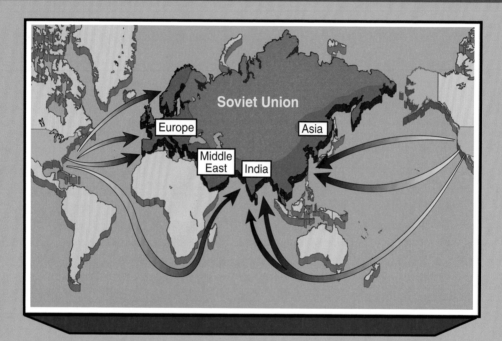

Source: Harold J. Clem, "Global Power Pattern Theories," National Defense University, 2007. www.ndu.edu.

- When Palestinians held democratic elections in January 2006, the Islamic fundamentalist group **Hamas**, which has said it favors the destruction of Israel, won a landslide victory.

- The day after Iranian president Mahmoud Ahmadinejad stated that Israel should be wiped off the map, Israeli prime minister Ariel Sharon called for Iran to be **expelled** from the United Nations.

Main Points of the Bush Doctrine

In response to the attacks of September 11, 2001, on September 17, 2002, President George W. Bush presented a national security strategy that came to be known as the Bush Doctrine. In his own words, the president explains the four main points of the Bush Doctrine.

Pre-emption: "The United States has long maintained the option of preemptive actions to counter a sufficient threat to our national security. The greater the threat, the greater is the risk of inaction. . . . To forestall or prevent. . . hostile acts by our adversaries, the United States will, if necessary, act preemptively."

Act Unilaterally: "While the United States will constantly strive to enlist the support of the international community [to fight terrorism], we will not hesitate to act alone, if necessary, to exercise our right of self defense."

Maintain Strength Beyond Challenge: "We must build and maintain our defenses beyond challenge. Our military's highest priority is to defend the United States . . . and decisively defeat any adversary if deterrence fails."

Extend Democracy: "Freedom is the non-negotiable demand of human dignity; the birthright of every person–in every civilization. Throughout history, freedom has been threatened by war and terror; it has been challenged by the clashing wills of powerful states and the evil designs of tyrants. . . . Today, humanity holds in its hands the opportunity to further freedom's triumph over these foes. The United States welcomes our responsibility to lead in this great mission."

Source: George W. Bush, "The National Security Strategy of the United States of America," White House, September 20, 2002. www.whitehouse.gov.

Global Military Spending

The Bush Doctrine requires strength beyond challenge, meaning that the United States supports the largest military force in the world in order to maintain its sole superpower status. This chart shows that the United States spends nearly 7 times more on its military budget than Russia, 8 times more than China, and nearly 50 times more than North Korea and Iran.

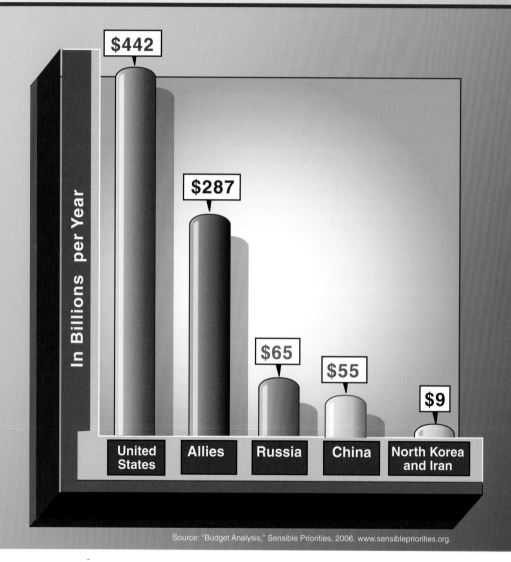

Source: "Budget Analysis," Sensible Priorities, 2006. www.sensiblepriorities.org.

Nuclear Sites Inside Iran

Iran began building nuclear facilities in the late 1980s. While the United States maintains Iran is planning to build nuclear weapons, Iranian leaders say they are only constructing nuclear power plants. This map shows various Iranian nuclear sites that may be used either for peaceful capabilities or for making nuclear bombs.

Source: "Iran's Nuclear Related Sites," Center for Nonproliferation Studies, 2007. http://cns.miis.edu.

- In 2002, Iran confirmed to the International Atomic Energy Agency that it was building two **uranium** enrichment plants and a heavy-water production facility. These facilities can be used to make fuel for either nuclear power plants or weapons.

- According to the National Security Strategy published by the White House, **Iran** sponsors terrorism, threatens Israel, and seeks to thwart Middle East peace.

What Effect Has the Iraq War Had on National Security?

"The war on terror cannot be won if we fail in Iraq."

—George W. Bush, "Renewal in Iraq."

"There is no better example of the folly and reckless ambition of the Bush administration than the misguided decision to invade and occupy Iraq."

—Craig R. Eisendrath and Melvin A. Goodman, *Bush League Diplomacy.*

In October 2001, weeks after the terrorist attacks in New York and Washington, D.C., the United States went to war in Afghanistan to capture terrorist mastermind Osama bin Laden, destroy al Qaeda training camps, and depose the fundamentalist Taliban government. The Taliban was routed within a month, but Bin Laden escaped into the rugged mountain terrain along the Pakistan border. Although democratic elections were later held with the oversight of the United States, most of Afghanistan remained in a state of chaos, with warlords from various factions controlling the countryside. While large numbers of al Qaeda and the Taliban were killed or forced to flee, many remained among the civilian population and slowly began to rebuild their organizations in the Waziristan region of Pakistan.

In the months following the U.S. victory in Afghanistan, the attentions of the Bush administration turned to Iraqi leader Saddam Hussein, who was said to be threatening national security by building weapons of mass destruction (WMD). It was also inferred that Hussein was helping terrorists in general and had provided aid to those who carried out the 9/11 attacks in the United States. Critics of the administration argued that UN weapons inspectors could find no WMD in Iraq and that there was no proven connection between Hussein and 9/11 or the al Qaeda terrorist group. However, the administration convinced the public that Hussein was a threat, and by early 2003, 62 percent of Americans supported military action to force Saddam Hussein from power.

> " Although democratic elections were later held with the oversight of the United States, most of Afghanistan remained in a state of chaos, with warlords from various factions controlling the countryside. "

"We Must Succeed in Iraq"

On March 20, 2003, the Iraq War began when American bombs rained down on Baghdad. By May 1 the end of major combat was announced, Saddam Hussein had been deposed, and the United States began its long occupation of Iraq. In the years that followed, the United States oversaw several democratic elections and the implementation of an Iraqi constitution. However, the occupation went badly for the United States, and the situation in Iraq deteriorated into a sectarian civil war between Sunni and Shiite religious factions. American soldiers were caught in the middle. By 2007 the situation was so dire that two out of three Americans supported a withdrawal from Iraq, but Bush continued to link the war in Iraq to America's national security. On a nationally televised speech on January 10, 2007, the president stated:

> Tonight in Iraq, the Armed Forces of the United States are engaged in a struggle that will determine the direction of the global war on terror—and our safety here at home. . . . The consequences of failure are clear: Radical Islamic extremists would grow in strength and gain new recruits.

They would be in a better position to topple moderate governments, create chaos in the region, and use oil revenues to fund their ambitions. . . . Our enemies would have a safe haven from which to plan and launch attacks on the American people. On September the 11th, 2001, we saw what a refuge for extremists on the other side of the world could bring to the streets of our own cities. For the safety of our people, America must succeed in Iraq.[45]

"The U.S. Caught in a Quagmire"

Despite Bush's claims, a considerable number of foreign policy experts have asserted that the war increased international terrorism, therefore making the United States less safe. In March 2007 *Los Angeles Times* op-ed columnist Rosa Brooks discussed some of these issues:

We've seen the war in Iraq fuel anti-U.S. sentiment worldwide; we've seen copycat suicide bombings increase in Afghanistan; we've seen the Iraq conflict further inflame tensions with Iran and throughout the Middle East; we've seen hostile states around the globe emboldened by the image of the U.S. caught in a quagmire; we've seen Al Qaeda regroup; we've seen Iraq become a top training ground for aspiring terrorists from all over.[46]

> **The attentions of the Bush administration turned to Iraqi leader Saddam Hussein, who was said to be threatening national security by building weapons of mass destruction.**

Costs of the War

Whether the Iraq War has made the United States safer has been a subject of persistent debate since the war began in 2003. But the situation in Iraq is extremely complex and has influenced two major areas of national security: the economy and military readiness.

In economic terms, the war has played a part in creating one of the largest budget deficits in U.S. history. And the expense of the war has been much higher than originally stated. For example, in late 2002 Mitch Daniels, director of the Office of Management and Budget, said that the war would cost between $50 billion and $60 billion. In March 2003, days before the war began, Deputy Defense Secretary Paul Wolfowitz told the House Appropriations Committee that the war would pay for itself with Iraqi oil revenues, which were projected to bring in between $50 billion and $100 billion over the course of several years. That revenue never materialized because Iraq's oil infrastructure, which was in bad shape at the start of the war, has been continually damaged by sabotage, combat, and acts of terrorism since the U.S. invasion.

Despite the optimistic projections, by March 2007 the war in Iraq had cost American taxpayers approximately $318.5 billion —that is $2 billion a week, $285 million a day, or $100,000 per minute. While these figures represent money already spent, economists have figured that total expenditures for the war might someday reach anywhere from $1 trillion to $2 trillion if, as Defense Department planners say, a large U.S. force remains in the country until 2010. This figure includes large future outlays to pay soldiers and civilian contractors, replace military hardware such as tanks, munitions, helicopters, Humvees, and countless other expenses. In addition, reconstruction of Iraq's damaged infrastructure could add another $250 billion to the final price tag.

> **Whether the Iraq War has made the United States safer has been a subject of persistent debate since the war began in 2003.**

The human cost of the war is also extremely expensive both in pain and suffering for soldiers and in monetary terms. As of March 2007 over 16,000 soldiers had been wounded in Iraq. Because of improvements from previous wars in battlefield medicine and body armor, many more soldiers with major injuries survived. According to the Pentagon, about 20 percent of those injured have suffered major head or spinal injury and 6 percent are amputees. Another 21 percent suffered serious wounds, including blindness, deafness, nerve damage, and burns. In addition, 30 percent of U.S. troops have developed mental health problems within three to four months of returning from Iraq. The medical costs of caring for these men and women is enormous. A single Iraq War veteran with brain injuries is projected to cost the government $5 million over the next 20 years. In all, economists believe that total health costs will add up to $250 billion.

Deficit Spending

Whatever the actual total cost, the Iraq War has largely been paid for with borrowed money because, unlike previous major wars, the government cut taxes at the same time it increased military spending. As Richard Kogan, a senior fellow at the Center on Budget and Policy Priorities, a think tank in Washington, D.C., says, "It's fair to say all of the money spent on the war has been borrowed. But eventually everything has to be paid for."[47]

Since the beginning of the war, the government has borrowed between $318 billion and $413 billion each year. Most of this money has been lent to the United States by China. This is troublesome to those who believe that this situation gives China great power over the United States. As Indiana senator Evan Bayh said in March 2006:

> "Deputy Defense Secretary Paul Wolfowitz told the House Appropriations Committee that the war would pay for itself with Iraqi oil revenues, which were projected to bring in between $50 billion and $100 billion over the course of several years."

> We need to take a serious look at the debt we are piling up with foreign countries because with every additional dollar we owe, we are giving up another piece of our national sovereignty. The more of our debt these foreign governments control, the more leverage they will have at the negotiating table on issues like trade, currency, and even national security.[48]

In one nightmare scenario, China could convert its vast holdings of U.S. dollars to the European currency, the euro, or to the Japanese yen. This would cause the dollar to collapse, as retired brigadier general Victor N. Corpus explains:

Once the dollar is rejected in favor of the euro or another currency for global oil transactions, the dollar will rapidly lose its value and central banks all over the world will be racing to diversify to other currencies. The shift . . . will have a devastating effect on the dollar. It could cause the dollar to collapse; and the whole US economy crashing down with it—a scene reminiscent of the collapse of the Twin Towers on September 11, 2001. But this one will be a thousand times more devastating. A successful assault on the US dollar will make America crawl on its knees with a minimum of movements.[49]

Effect on Military Readiness

In addition to financial costs, critics of the war argue the Iraq War damages national security because of its impact on the U.S. armed forces. According to the Pentagon, nearly one-third of the troops in Iraq have served multiple tours of duty, each lasting one year. Most of these men and women must patrol the dangerous streets of Iraqi cities wearing 50 to 60 pounds of full battle gear as temperatures climb, often to 120 degrees. Of these soldiers, 94 percent have been shot at and 86 percent know someone who has been killed or severely wounded. As a result, military morale reached an all-time low by 2007, when a Zogby poll showed 72 percent of American troops serving in Iraq said the United States should exit that country within the next year. More than one in four said the troops should leave immediately.

> " **Economists have figured that total expenditures for the war might someday reach anywhere from $1 trillion to $2 trillion.** "

Such attitudes have hurt efforts to recruit new soldiers, and the military has fallen short of its recruiting goals despite doubling enlistment bonuses, increasing the top age for recruits, and accepting a higher number of high school dropouts and those with criminal records. Because of a shortage of new soldiers and the strain of repeated tours of duty on enlisted personnel, Pennsylvania congressman John Murtha has published the following conclusion:

The U.S. Army's preparedness for war has eroded to levels not witnessed by our country in decades. As deployments to Iraq . . . continue unabated, there is a very real prospect that Army readiness will continue to erode, undermining its ability to meet the theater commanders' needs and foreclosing any option for the U.S. to respond to conflicts elsewhere around the globe. The degradation of Army readiness is primarily a function of unanticipated high troop deployment levels to Iraq, chronic equipment and personnel shortages, funding constraints, and Pentagon civilian mismanagement.[50]

> **A single Iraq War veteran with brain injuries is projected to cost the government $5 million over the next 20 years.**

In February 2007 defense secretary Robert Gates agreed with Murtha's assessment. However, Gates stated that the increased military budget proposed by Bush for 2008 would solve many of the problems facing the military. With more money, the Department of Defense would continue to:

> sustain the all-volunteer military by reducing stress on the force and improving the quality of life for our troops and their families; to improve readiness through additional training and maintenance, and . . . fund U.S. military operations in Iraq, Afghanistan and elsewhere in the ongoing campaign against violent jihadist networks around the globe.[51]

Al Qaeda Rebuilding

With military resources stretched thin by the Iraq War, America's enemies know it would be difficult for the United States to respond to crises elsewhere. Such is the case in Pakistan, where in February 2007 al Qaeda had reorganized and was said to be planning more deadly strikes against the United States and its allies. According to Bruce Hoffman, a senior fellow at West Point's Combating Terrorism Center:

Rather than being degraded to the point that it can threaten only softer, more accessible targets like hotels and mass transit, Al Qaeda is very much sticking with its classic playbook of simultaneous, spectacular strikes against even hardened objectives. In other words, we have more to fear from this resilient organization, not less.[52]

Hoffman says that al Qaeda's leadership was able to plan this major resurgence because the Iraq War has consumed so many U.S. military, intelligence, and economic resources. Like many other terrorism analysts, Hoffman believes the war in Iraq has made the United States less safe. With an unpredictable situation in the Middle East continuing to challenge the national security of the United States, the role played by the war in Iraq will undoubtedly fuel debate for many years to come.

Primary Source Quotes*

What Effect Has the Iraq War Had on National Security?

❝Success in Iraq remains critical to our national security and to success in the War on Terror.❞

—National Security Council, "Highlights of the Iraq Strategy Review," January 2007. www.whitehouse.gov.

The National Security Council is part of the executive branch of government responsible for coordinating policy on national security issues.

❝Millions of conservatives across this nation believe this war was unconstitutional, unaffordable, and worst of all, unnecessary. It was waged against an evil man, but one who had a total military budget only two-tenths of 1 percent of ours.❞

—John J. Duncan Jr., "The War In Iraq," U.S. House of Representatives, June 16, 2006. www.house.gov.

Duncan is a U.S. congressman from Tennessee.

Bracketed quotes indicate conflicting positions.

* Editor's Note: While the definition of a primary source can be narrowly or broadly defined, for the purposes of Compact Research, a primary source consists of: 1) results of original research presented by an organization or researcher; 2) eyewitness accounts of events, personal experience, or work experience; 3) first-person editorials offering pundits' opinions; 4) government officials presenting political plans and/or policies; 5) representatives of organizations presenting testimony or policy.

66 Let's be clear. U.S. forces are in Iraq to help the Iraqis fight the terrorists there, so we don't have to fight them here in the United States. . . . Quitting is not an exit strategy. It would be a formula for putting the American people at still greater risk. 99

—Donald H. Rumsfeld, "News Briefing with Secretary of Defense Donald Rumsfeld and General Peter Pace," Department of Defense, November 29, 2005. www.defenselink.mil.

Rumsfeld was the secretary of defense from 2001 to 2006.

66 If every American taxpayer had to submit an extra five or ten thousand dollars to the IRS this April to pay for the war, I'm quite certain it would end very quickly. 99

—Ron Paul, "Inflation and War Finance," SafeHaven, January 29, 2007. www.safehaven.com.

Paul is a U.S. congressman from Texas.

66 Our troops are counting on their elected leaders in Washington, D.C. to provide them with the support they need to do their mission. We have a responsibility . . . to make sure that our men and women in uniform have the resources . . . they need to prevail. 99

—George W. Bush, "Press Conference by the President," February 14, 2007. www.whitehouse.gov.

Bush is the forty-third president of the United States.

66 [If] we leave Iraq before the mission is completed, the enemy is going to come after us. Having seen our interests attacked repeatedly over the years, and knowing the ambitions of the terrorists, this nation has made a decision: We will engage these enemies. We will face them far from home, so we do not have to face them on the streets of our own cities. 99

—Richard Cheney, "Vice President's Remarks at a Rally for the Troops," February 21, 2007. www.whitehouse.gov.

Cheney is the forty-sixth vice president of the United States.

66 The idea that, because our troops are in Iraq, terrorists will only attack us there and not 'in the streets of our own cities' is, first and foremost, an insult to our troops because it treats them as if their entire mission is to serve as bait for terrorists. That's not what our troops— or America—was told this [war] was all about. 99

—David Sirota, "Iraq, London, & America's Homeland Security," Sirotablog, July 7, 2005. www.davidsirota.com.

Sirota is a political journalist, best-selling author, and senior editor of *In These Times* magazine.

66 Going deeper into debt to China and Japan undermines our economy, our national security, and is deeply irresponsible to our children who must one day pay our bills with interest. 99

—Evan Bayh, "Economic Policy: Federal Deficit," March 16, 2006. http://bayh.senate.gov.

Bayh is a U.S. senator from Indiana.

66 **America's military is approaching a crisis that could rival the one it faced at the end of the Vietnam War. George Bush's reckless invasion of Iraq and the resulting occupation have stretched our armed forces to the breaking point.** 99

—Tod Ensign, *America's Military Today: The Challenge of Militarism*. New York: New Press, 2004, p. ix.

Ensign is the director of Citizen Soldier, a nonprofit GI rights advocacy group.

66 **Two hundred thousand [American soldiers] are in the Gulf region, another 200,000 are in Afghanistan, leaving about 2 million Americans still available, with the vast fleet and air forces that we have, to respond to any other challenge that might come our way.** 99

—Peter Pace, "Gates, Pace Give Update on Iraq, Afghanistan, Readiness," U.S. Department of Defense, February 15, 2007. www.defenselink.mil.

Pace was appointed chairman of the Joint Chiefs of Staff in September 2005.

66 **The Army has become a 'hand-to-mouth' organization. Its inability to get ahead of the deployment and training curves is rooted in the Administration's miscalculations and blind optimism about troop . . . requirements for the U.S. occupation of Iraq. The consequent failure to plan has forced the Army to play catch-up ever since the fall of Baghdad.** 99

—John Murtha, "United States Army Military Readiness," September 13, 2006. www.house.gov.

Murtha is a U.S. congressman from Pennsylvania.

66 **[This Army is] the best led, trained and equipped Army that I've ever seen in the field.** 99

—Peter J. Schoolmaker, "The Best Led, Trained, and Equipped Army," Department of Defense, November 26, 2006. www.defenselink.mil.

Schoolmaker is chief of staff of the U.S. Army.

Facts and Illustrations

What Effect Has the Iraq War Had on National Security?

- The United States **defeated** the Taliban government in Afghanistan within a month, but some members of al Qaeda escaped to re-form the terrorist organization in Waziristan, Pakistan.

- In early 2003, **62 percent** of Americans supported military action to force Saddam Hussein from power.

- The United States invaded Iraq on **March 20, 2003**, and major combat operations ended by May 1.

- By 2007 **two out of three** Americans supported a U.S. withdrawal from Iraq.

- President Bush repeatedly stated that the **Iraq War** was necessary to ensure United States national security.

- By March 2007 the war in Iraq had cost American taxpayers approximately **$400 billion**—that is $2 billion a week, $285 million a day, or $100,000 per minute.

- As of March 2007 over **16,000** soldiers had been wounded in Iraq.

- Economists believe that total health costs for wounded Iraq War veterans will add up to **$250 billion**.

Map of Iraq

The United States invaded Iraq in March 2003, deposing Saddam Hussein in Baghdad. Since that time, American forces have engaged in major battles with insurgents in Fallujah, Tikrit, Najaf, and Basra in the south.

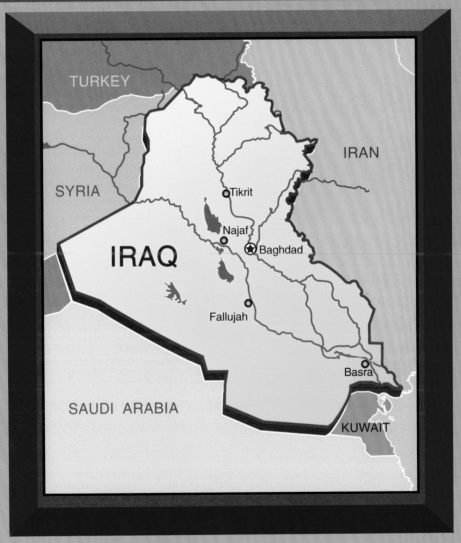

Source: "Defend America," Department of Defense, 2007. www.defendamerica.mil.

A Significant Increase in Global Terrorism

The number of international terrorist attacks has grown considerably since the beginning of the Iraq War. This graph shows a decline of terrorist acts between 1999 and 2002, with a fourfold increase by radical Islamic extremists since 2003. This is the largest increase in terrorist activity ever recorded since the CIA started keeping records in 1968.

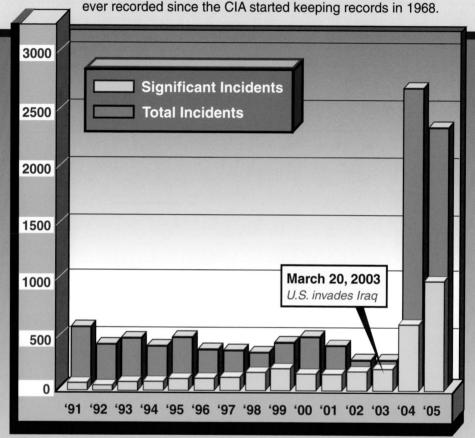

Source: Larry C. Johnson, "The Facts Behind the NIE," No Quarter, September 26, 2006. http://noquarter.typepad.com.

- Since the beginning of the war, the government has borrowed between **$318 billion** and **$413 billion** each year.

- The Iraq War has largely been paid for with **borrowed money** because unlike previous major wars, the government cut taxes at the same time it increased military spending.

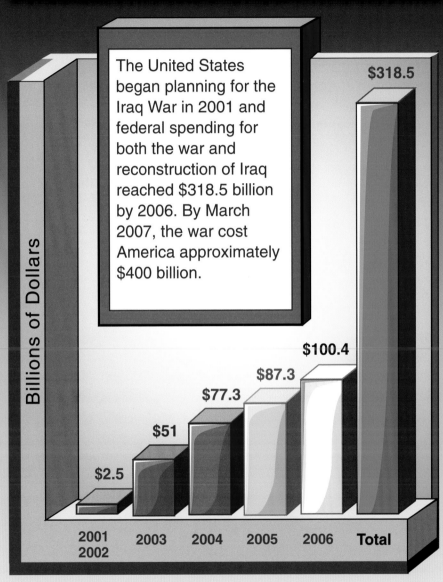

The Cost of the Iraq War and Reconstruction

The United States began planning for the Iraq War in 2001 and federal spending for both the war and reconstruction of Iraq reached $318.5 billion by 2006. By March 2007, the war cost America approximately $400 billion.

$318.5

$100.4

$87.3

$77.3

$51

$2.5

Billions of Dollars

2001 2002   2003   2004   2005   2006   Total

Source: The Foundation for National Progress, 2007.

- According to the Pentagon, the U.S. Army's preparedness has eroded to levels not witnessed in **decades** because of the Iraq War.

Confronting Terrorism

"Will the United States be safer from terrorism if it confronts the countries and groups that promote terrorism in the MIddle East, or will the United States be safer from terrorism if it stays out of other countries' affairs in the Middle East?"

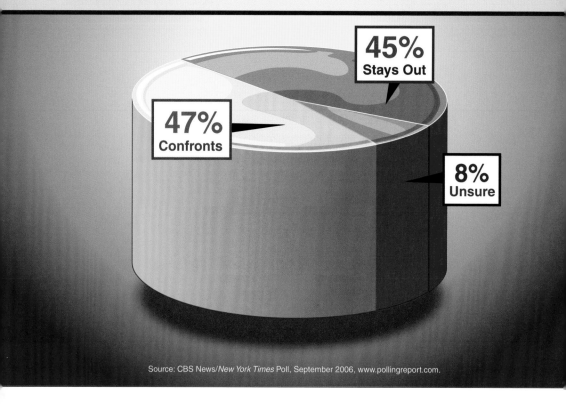

45%
Stays Out

47%
Confronts

8%
Unsure

Source: CBS News/*New York Times* Poll, September 2006, www.pollingreport.com.

Key People and Advocacy Groups

Mahmoud Ahmadinejad: As the president of Iran, Ahmadinejad controls about 10 percent of the world's known oil reserves. Ahmadinejad is also an outspoken critic of the United States and has threatened to wipe Israel off the map. American intelligence forces say Ahmadinejad is using Iran's vast oil wealth to develop nuclear weapons and ballistic missiles that might some day be used against Israel, Saudi Arabia, or Western Europe.

John Ashcroft: As the attorney general of the United States when the 9/11 strikes occurred, Ashcroft was in charge of responding to those attacks. Ashcroft has been a staunch defender of the Patriot Act, NSA eavesdropping, and other controversial measures taken in the war on terror.

Osama bin Laden: A devoted Muslim from an early age, Bin Laden grew up in an extremely wealthy family in Yemen. In 1980 after the Soviet Union invaded Afghanistan, Bin Laden used his money to recruit, finance, and train an estimated 35,000 non-Afghan mercenaries who opposed the Soviets. In the 1980s, in collaboration with the U.S. Central Intelligence Agency, Bin Laden built training camps in Afghanistan to train fighters in anti-Soviet terrorist techniques. By 1996 these camps were providing terrorist training to anti-American terrorists who would attack U.S. targets.

George W. Bush: As the 43rd president of the United States, Bush oversaw the response to the terrorist attacks of September 11, 2001, and was commander in chief during the Afghanistan and Iraq wars. Bush was instrumental in creating the Department of Homeland Security and was the driving force behind the passage of the Patriot Act and the Military Commissions Act.

Richard B. Cheney: As the 46th vice president, Cheney exerted great influence in the Bush administration as one of the leading proponents of the Patriot Act, the 2003 invasion of Iraq, and the use of extreme interrogation techniques against alleged terrorists. Cheney is often described as one of the most powerful vice presidents in history.

Stephen E. Flynn: A former Coast Guard commander, Flynn is currently the senior fellow for national security studies at the Council on Foreign Relations. Flynn is an adviser on homeland security for the U.S. Commission on National Security and author of *America the Vulnerable* and *Edge of Disaster*. His fields of expertise include catastrophic terrorism, maritime transportation security, border control modernization, and critical infrastructure protection.

Alberto Gonzales: Gonzales was appointed White House counsel by President George W. Bush in 2001 and was made attorney general of the United States in 2005. As White House counsel, Gonzales wrote a memo stating that international laws against torture do not apply to those the president has labeled enemy combatants. Gonzales also authored the presidential order authorizing military tribunals for terrorism suspects.

Michael V. Hayden: An air force general, Hayden was director of the National Security Agency from 1999 to 2005, during which time he oversaw the program of warrantless wiretapping of people in the United States suspected of working with purported terrorist groups. Hayden was made director of the Central Intelligence Agency on May 30, 2006.

Robert Swan Mueller III: Named director of the Federal Bureau of Investigation just one week before the 9/11 terrorist strikes, Mueller directed a massive reorganization of the FBI in order to focus the bureau's resources on counterterrorism.

Peter Pace: Sworn in as 16th chairman of the Joint Chiefs of Staff on September 30, 2005, Pace, a U.S. Marine Corps general, served as the principal military adviser to the president, the secretary of defense, and the National Security Council. Pace is the first marine to serve as chairman. He also holds the distinction of being the first marine to have served as the vice chairman.

David H. Petraeus: As the commander of the army's 101st Airborne Division Petraeus participated in the initial invasion of Iraq and later focused on political and economic reconstruction efforts. In 2007 Petraeus was named commander of Multinational Force Iraq, the post that oversees all U.S. forces in Iraq.

al Qaeda: Al Qaeda, whose name translates as "the law," or "the base," is one of the most well-known terrorist organizations in the world. Founded by Osama bin Laden, members of al Qaeda operate out of independent cells in several countries. Al Qaeda has taken credit for several high-profile terrorist acts, including the strikes on the World Trade Center and Pentagon on September 11, 2001.

Condoleeza Rice: As the assistant to the president for national security affairs, or national security adviser, Rice helped plan the U.S. invasion of Iraq. In January 2005 Rice was named 66th secretary of state. She is the first African American woman to hold that job.

Donald Rumsfeld: Rumsfeld served as secretary of defense twice, once under President Gerald Ford from 1975 to 1977 and later under George W. Bush from 2001 to 2006. Rumsfeld led the military planning and execution of the U.S. invasion of Afghanistan and the 2003 invasion of Iraq. Rumsfeld sent as small a force as possible to both conflicts, a controversial concept known as the Rumsfeld Doctrine.

Chronology

1945
The United Nations is founded with the stated purpose of helping nations avoid the "scourge of war."

1998
February: Bin Laden issues a fatwa in an Arabic-language newspaper in London stating that Muslims should consider it their holy duty to kill any Americans, anywhere on earth.

1991
December 8: The Cold War ends as the Soviet Union is dissolved and replaced by the Commonwealth of Independent States.

1945   1975   1990   2000

1978
Congress passes the Foreign Intelligence Surveillance Act (FISA) to regulate the tactics that intelligence agencies may use to investigate individuals in the interest of national security.

2001
September 10: Attorney General John Ashcroft proposes massive budget cuts for the Federal Bureau of Investigation's counterterrorism division.

September 11: In the worst terrorist attack in American history, 3,000 Americans are killed as 19 terrorists destroy the World Trade Center, badly damage the Pentagon, and crash a plane into a field in Pennsylvania.

October 26: President George W. Bush signs the USA PATRIOT Act, an all-encompassing anti-terrorism bill that grants government authorities broad powers to investigate Americans.

November 13: The Bush administration issues a military order that grants sweeping powers to the military to arrest and detain anyone suspected of terrorism against the United States, its citizens, its national security, foreign policy, or economy.

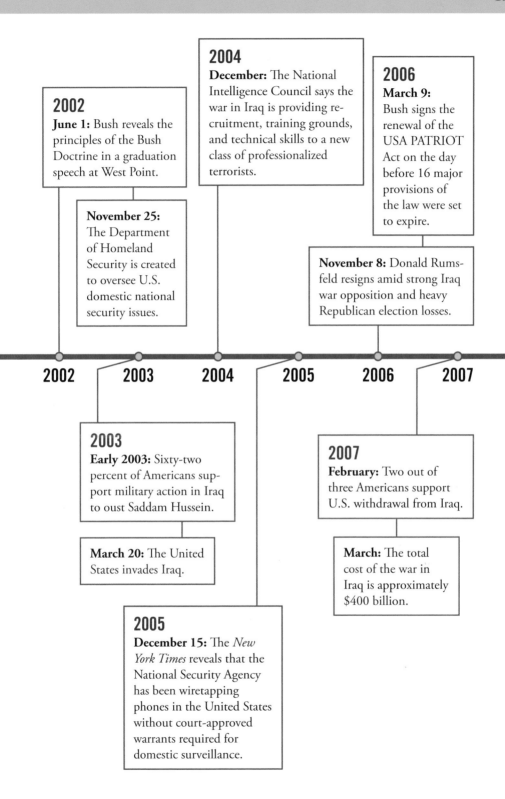

2002
June 1: Bush reveals the principles of the Bush Doctrine in a graduation speech at West Point.

November 25: The Department of Homeland Security is created to oversee U.S. domestic national security issues.

2004
December: The National Intelligence Council says the war in Iraq is providing recruitment, training grounds, and technical skills to a new class of professionalized terrorists.

2006
March 9: Bush signs the renewal of the USA PATRIOT Act on the day before 16 major provisions of the law were set to expire.

November 8: Donald Rumsfeld resigns amid strong Iraq war opposition and heavy Republican election losses.

2002   2003   2004   2005   2006   2007

2003
Early 2003: Sixty-two percent of Americans support military action in Iraq to oust Saddam Hussein.

March 20: The United States invades Iraq.

2007
February: Two out of three Americans support U.S. withdrawal from Iraq.

March: The total cost of the war in Iraq is approximately $400 billion.

2005
December 15: The *New York Times* reveals that the National Security Agency has been wiretapping phones in the United States without court-approved warrants required for domestic surveillance.

Related Organizations

American Civil Liberties Union (ACLU)

125 Broad St., 18th Fl., New York, NY 10004-2400

phone: (212) 549-2500

e-mail: aclu@aclu.org • Web site: www.aclu.org

The ACLU is a national organization that works to defend civil rights as guaranteed in the Constitution. The "Spyfiles" division of the organization is dedicated to monitoring the roles that the Pentagon, the NSA, and the FBI take in spying on American citizens. The ACLU makes various reports, legal documents, and news releases available on its Web site along with the triannual newsletter *Civil Liberties*, and a set of handbooks on individual rights.

Center for National Security Studies

1120 19th St. NW, 8th Fl., Washington, DC 20036

phone: (202) 721-5650 • fax: (202) 530-0128

e-mail: cnss@gwu.edu • Web site: www.cnss.org

The mission of the Center for National Security Studies is to prevent claims of national security from eroding civil liberties or constitutional rights and to limit the powers of the FBI and CIA. The center partners with the National Security Archive, the most successful nonprofit user of the U.S. Freedom of Information Act and the largest nongovernmental collector of declassified U.S. documents. The center publishes dozens of documents and reports pertaining to intelligence agencies and civil liberties on its Web site.

Department of Homeland Security (DHS)

Washington, DC 20528

Web site: www.dhs.gov

The Department of Homeland Security (DHS) was created by the federal government in 2002 to secure the homeland from terrorist attacks. The mission of the DHS is to identify and understand threats, assess vulnerabilities, determine potential impacts, and disseminate timely information to security personnel and the American public. The DHS also is charged with leading national, state, local, and private-sector efforts to restore services and rebuild communities after acts of terrorism, natural disasters, or other emergencies.

Electronic Privacy Information Center (EPIC)

1718 Connecticut Ave. NW, Suite 200, Washington, DC 20009

phone: (202) 483-1140 • fax: (202) 483-1248

e-mail: info@epic.org • Web site: www.epic.org

EPIC is an organization that advocates the public's right to electronic privacy. It sponsors educational and research programs, compiles statistics, and conducts litigation. Its publications include the biweekly electronic newsletter *EPIC Alert* and dozens of online reports and books concerning civil liberties, privacy, and government spying.

Federal Bureau of Investigation (FBI)

935 Pennsylvania Ave. NW, Rm. 7972, Washington, DC 20535

phone: (202) 324-3000

Web site: www.fbi.gov

The FBI, the principal investigative arm of the U.S. Department of Justice, has the authority and responsibility to investigate and prevent terrorism. The FBI also is authorized to provide other law enforcement agencies with fingerprint identification, laboratory examinations, and police training. The mission of the FBI is to uphold the law through the investigation of violations of federal criminal law; to protect the United States from foreign intelligence and terrorist activities; to provide leadership and law enforcement assistance to federal, state, local, and international agencies; and to perform these responsibilities in a manner that is responsive to the needs of the public and faithful to the Constitution of the United States. Press releases, congressional statements, and major speeches on issues concerning the FBI are available on the agency's Web site.

National Priorities Project (NPP)

17 New South St., Northampton, MA 01060

phone: (413) 584-9556 • fax: (413) 586-9647

e-mail: pschwartz@nationalpriorities.org

Web site: http://nationalpriorities.org

The NPP provides data on the impact of federal spending policies for states, cities, and counties, and educates and trains activists and elected officials on the federal budget. Publications include reports about federal spending in each state, e-mail alerts, and the Web-based reports *Where Do Your Tax Dollars Go? Cost of Iraq War Rises for American Taxpayers*, and *Better Security for Less Money*.

National Security Agency

9800 Savage Rd., Ft. Meade, MD 20755-6248

(301) 688-6524

Web site: www.nsa.gov

The National Security Agency coordinates, directs, and performs activities, such as designing cipher systems, which protect American information systems and produce foreign intelligence information. The NSA employs satellites to collect data from telephones and computers, aiding in the fight against terrorism. Speeches, briefings, and reports are available on its Web site.

Project on Government Oversight (POGO)

66 11th St. NW, Suite 500, Washington, DC 20001-4542

(202) 347-1122 • fax: (202) 347-1116

e-mail: info@pogo.org • Web site: www.pogo.org

Founded in 1981, the Project on Government Oversight investigates and exposes corruption and misconduct within the federal government. Those investigations focus on the Department of Homeland Security, the Defense Department, the FBI, and other federal agencies charged with protecting the public. POGO publishes a blog, press alerts, investigative reports, a federal contractor misconduct database, and e-mail updates.

Project on Government Secrecy

Federation of American Scientists

1717 K St. NW, Suite 209, Washington, DC 20036

(202) 454-4691 • fax: (202) 675-1010

e-mail: saftergood@fas.org • Web site: www.fas.org/pgs

The Project on Government Secrecy program of the Federation of American Scientists (FAS) seeks to reduce the threat to the United States, and to the world, from biological, conventional, and nuclear weapons. Endorsed by 67 Nobel laureates in chemistry, economics, medicine, and physics, FAS brings a scientific perspective to public policy.

For Further Research

Books

Leigh Armistead, *Information Operations: Warfare and the Hard Reality of Soft Power*. Washington, DC: Brassey's, 2004.

Martha Baer et al., *Safe: The Race to Protect Ourselves in a Newly Dangerous World*. New York: HarperCollins, 2005.

Carol Brightman, *Total Insecurity: The Myth of American Omnipotence*. New York: Verso, 2004.

Matthew Brzezinski, *Fortress America: On the Front Lines of Homeland Security—an Inside Look at the Coming Surveillance State*. New York: Bantam, 2004.

David B. Cohen and John W. Wells, eds., *American National Security and Civil Liberties in an Era of Terrorism*. New York: Palgrave Macmillan, 2004.

William Crotty, ed., *The Politics of Terror: The U.S. Response to 9/11*. Boston: Northeastern University Press, 2004.

Craig R. Eisendrath and Melvin A. Goodman, *Bush League Diplomacy: How the Neoconservatives Are Putting the World at Risk*. Amherst, NY: Prometheus, 2004.

Tod Ensign, *America's Military Today: The Challenge of Militarism*. New York: New Press, 2004.

Stephen Flynn, *America the Vulnerable: How Our Government Is Failing to Protect Us from Terrorism*. New York: HarperCollins, 2004.

David Hunt, *They Just Don't Get It: How Washington Is Still Compromising Your Safety—and What You Can Do About It*. New York: Crown Forum, 2005.

Thomas H. Kean et al., *The 9/11 Commission Report: Final Report of the National Commission on Terrorist Attacks upon the United States*. New York: Norton, 2004.

Robert Latham, ed., *Bombs and Bandwidth: The Emerging Relationship Between Information Technology and Security.* New York: New Press, 2003.

Michael C. Ruppert, *Crossing the Rubicon: The Decemberline of the American Empire at the End of the Age of Oil.* Gabriola, BC: New Society, 2004.

Martin Schram, *Avoiding Armageddon: Our Future, Our Choice; Companion to the PBS Series from Ted Turner Documentaries.* New York: Basic Books, 2003.

Cynthia A. Watson, *U.S. National Security.* Santa Barbara: ABC-CLIO, 2002.

Alan P. Zelicoff and Michael Bellomo, *Microbe: Are We Ready for the Next Plague?* New York: American Management Association, 2005.

Periodicals

Martin Edwin Andersen, "Is Torture an Option in War on Terror? Interrogators Increasingly Frustrated with Hardened al-Qaeda Terrorists Are Considering the Use of Tactics Once Unthinkable for U.S. Law-Enforcement Officers," *Insight on the News*, June 17, 2002.

Atlantic Monthly, "Nuclear Iran: The *Atlantic* Recently Asked a Group of Foreign-Policy Authorities About Iran's Nuclear Quest," September 2006.

Holly Bailey, Richard Wolffe, and Evan Thomas, "Bush's Truman Show," *Newsweek*, February 12, 2007.

Elizabeth G. Book, "Nuke Explosion Would Make 'Nasty Cleanup,'" *National Defense*, June 2002.

Ashton Carter and Richard Lugar, "A New Era, a New Threat: The US and Russia Should Form a Coalition to Stop Terrorists Obtaining Nuclear Weapons," *Financial Times*, May 23, 2002.

Larry J. Dodgen, "Space and Missile Defense Strengthens the Joint War Fighter, Space and Missile Defense Command for National Security," *Army*, October 10, 2006.

Robert Dreyfuss and Dave Gilson, "Sunni, Shiite? . . . Anyone? Anyone?" *Mother Jones*, March/April 2007.

Michael Duffy, "What Would War Look Like?" *World*, September 25, 2006.

Energy, "Iran's Advantage: The Country Holds Ten Percent of the World's Proved Oil Reserves," Spring 2005.

Dan Ephron and Sarah Childress, "Forgotten Heroes," *Newsweek*, March 5, 2007.

David A. Fulghum and Douglas Barrie, "Busting the Bomb: Airmen and Politicians Ponder How to Decelerate Tehran's Development of Nuclear Weapons," *Aviation Week & Space Technology*, September 11, 2006.

Eugene Gholz, Daryl G. Press, and Benjamin Valentino, "Time to Offshore Our Troops," *New York Times*, December 12, 2006.

Duncan Graham-Rowe, "Electricity Grids Left Wide Open to Hackers," *New Scientist*, August 30, 2003.

Alain Gresh, "Middle East: What Will Emerge from the Ruins? As the Situation Escalated in the Middle East over the Summer, Some Pointed to World War III," *Catholic New Times*, September 10, 2006.

William F. Jasper, "Expanding Surveillance Authority: The Surveillance Power Demanded by President Bush Would Not Necessarily Provide Any Better Protection from Terrorism, but It Would Certainly Expand Executive Branch Power," *New American*, October 30, 2006.

Joshua Key, "Why I Fled George Bush's War (The Deserter's Tale: The Story of an Ordinary Soldier Who Walked Away from the War in Iraq)," *Maclean's*, February 5, 2007.

David Leonhard, "What $1 Trillion Can Buy (Besides the War in Iraq)," *New York Times Upfront*, February 19, 2007.

Charles Moskos, "Should the All Volunteer Force Be Replaced by Universal Mandatory National Service?" *Congressional Digest*, September 2006.

Norman J. Ornstein, "It's Armageddon: Who's in Charge Here?" *Fortune*, February 9, 2004.

Romesh Ratnesar and Elaine Shannon, "The Weight of the World (Secretary of State Condoleezza Rice and U.S. Foreign Policy)," *Time*, February 12, 2007.

John Steinbruner, "The Nuclear Impasse with Iran," *America*, July 3, 2006.

Scott Stossel, "North Korea: The War Game: Dealing with North Korea Could Make Iraq Look Like Child's Play—and the Longer We Wait, the Harder It Will Get," *Atlantic Monthly*, July/August 2005.

Internet Sources

ACLU, "NSA Spying on Americans Is Illegal," December 29, 2005. www.aclu.org/privacy/spying/23279res20051229.html.

Peter Bergen and Paul Cruickshank, "The Iraq Effect," *Mother Jones*, March 1, 2007. www.motherjones.com/news/featurex/2007/03/iraq_effect_1.html.

William J. Bicknell and Kenneth D. Bloem, "Smallpox and Bioterrorism: Why the Plan to Protect the Nation Is Stalled and What to Do," Cato Institute, September 5, 2003. www.cato.org/pubs/briefs/bp-085es.html.

John Murtha, "United States Army Military Readiness," September 13, 2006. www.house.gov/list/press/pa12_murtha/PRmilreadiness0913.html.

James A. Phillips, "National Security Isn't Just About Terrorism," Heritage Foundation, April 9, 2004. www.heritage.org/Research/National Security/wm472.cfm.

Source Notes

Overview

1. George H.W. Bush, "State of the Union Address," Infoplease, 2006. www.info please.com.
2. Matthew Brzezinski, *Fortress America: On the Front Lines of Homeland Security —an Inside Look at the Coming Surveillance State.* New York: Bantam, 2004, p. 13.
3. Cynthia A. Watson, *U.S. National Security.* Santa Barbara: ABC-CLIO, 2002, p.14.
4. Quoted in Cynthia A. Watson, *U.S. National Security*, p. 15.
5. Thomas H. Kean et al., *The 9/11 Commission Report: Final Report of the National Commission on Terrorist Attacks Upon the United States.* New York: Norton, 2004, p. 51.
6. George W. Bush, "President Discusses War on Terror," March 8, 2005. www. whitehouse.gov.
7. John Deutch and James R. Schlesinger, "National Security Consequences of U.S. Oil Dependency," New York: Council of Foreign Relations, 2006, pp. 3–4.
8. Cynthia A. Watson, *U.S. National Security,* pp. 8–9.

How Serious a Threat Is Terrorism to National Security?

9. Dale L. Watson, congressional testimony, FBI, February 6, 2002. www. fbi.gov.
10. Dale L. Watson, congressional testimony.
11. Kean et al., *The 9/11 Commission Report*, p. 48.
12. Robert Hutchings, National Intelligence Council, "Report of the National Intelligence Council's 2020 Project," December 2004. www.dni.gov.
13. Luke Mitchell, "A Run on Terror," *Harper's*, March 2004, p. 79.
14. Quoted in Jennifer Barrett, "Scared of Smallpox," MSNBC, October 28, 2001. www.msnbc.msn.com.
15. Robert Hutchings, National Intelligence Council, "Report of the National Intelligence Council's 2020 Project," December 2004. www.dni.gov.
16. Martin Schram, *Avoiding Armageddon: Our Future, Our Choice; Companion to the PBS Series from Ted Turner Documentaries.* New York: Basic Books, 2003, p. 200.
17. Quoted in Schram, *Avoiding Armageddon*, p. 203.
18. John Mintz, "Technical Hurdles Separate Terrorists from Biowarfare," *Washington Post*, December 30, 2004. www.washingtonpost.com.
19. Quoted in J. R. Nyquist, "Waiting for the Big One," *Financial Sense*, September 18, 2003. www.financialsense. com.
20. Graham Allison, "Dirty Bomb," PBS. org, February 2003. www.pbs.org.
21. John Mueller, "Is There Still a Terrorist Threat? The Myth of the Omnipresent Enemy," *Foreign Affairs*, September/October 2006. www.foreign affairs.org.

How Do National Security Concerns Affect Privacy Rights?

22. Supreme Court, "The Sedition Act of 1918," December 2006. www.pbs.org.
23. Quoted in Select Committee to Study Governmental Operations, Final Report. Washington, DC: Government

Printing Office, April 14, 1976, p. 2.

24. Cynthia A. Watson, *U.S. National Security*, pp. 3–4.

25. Quoted in Electronic Frontier Foundation, "Foreign Intelligence Surveillance Act," 2007. www.eff.org.

26. Marion E. Bowman, congressional testimony, FBI, July 31, 2002. www.fbi.gov.

27. Electronic Frontier Foundation, "Foreign Intelligence Surveillance Act."

28. Dan Eggen and Julie Tate, "U.S. Campaign Produces Few Convictions on Terrorism Charges," *Washington Post*, June 12, 2005. www.washingtonpost.com.

29. Quoted in Brian Wolly, "Wiretap Revelations Spur Presidential Powers Debate," PBS, March 28, 2006. www.pbs.org.

30. Al Gore, "The Full Text of Al Gore's Speech," *Huffington Post*, January 16, 2006. www.huffingtonpost.com.

31. Barton Gellman, Dafna Linzer, and Carol D. Leonnig, "NSA's Hunt for Terrorists Scrutinizes Thousands of Americans, but Most Are Later Cleared," *Washington Post*, February 5, 2006. www.washingtonpost.com.

32. Edward Kennedy, "On Wiretapping Bush Isn't Listening to the Constitution," *Boston Globe*, December 22, 2005. www.boston.com.

How Does U.S. Foreign Policy Affect National Security?

33. Quoted in Ian Shapiro, "Reopening the Case for Containment," *Los Angeles Times*, February 25, 2007, p. M3.

34. Harry Truman, "The Truman Doctrine," Yale Law School, 1997. www.yale.edu.

35. Quoted in Craig R. Eisendrath and Melvin A. Goodman, *Bush League Diplomacy*. Amherst, NY: Prometheus, 2004, p.17.

36. Eisendrath and Goodman, *Bush League Diplomacy*, p. 18.

37. Eisendrath and Goodman, *Bush League Diplomacy*, p. 23.

38. George W. Bush, "The National Security Strategy of the United States of America," White House, September 20, 2002. www.whitehouse.gov.

39. George W. Bush, "President Delivers Graduation Speech at West Point," White House, June 1, 2002. www.whitehouse.gov.

40. Shapiro, "Reopening the Case for Containment," p. M3.

41. United Nations, "Charter of the United Nations," 2007. www.un.org.

42. Quoted in Ken Silverstein, "Parties of God," *Harpers*, March 2007, p. 41.

43. Quoted in *Staff Report of the House Permanent Select Committee on Intelligence Subcommittee on Intelligence Policy*, "Recognizing Iran as a Strategic Threat: An Intelligence Challenge for the United States," August 23, 2006. www.intelligence.house.gov.

44. Quoted in Jorge Hirsh, "War Against Iran," antiwar.com, April 1, 2006. www.antiwar.com.

What Effect Has the Iraq War Had on National Security?

45. George W. Bush, "President Addresses the Nation," January 10, 2007. www.whitehouse.gov.

46. Rosa Brooks, "Up a Creek in a Swift Boat," *Los Angeles Times*, March 2, 2007, p. A23.

47. Quoted in Ron Scherer, "How US Is Deferring War Costs," *Christian Science Monitor*, January 16, 2006. www.csmonitor.com.

48. Evan Bayh, "Economic Policy: Federal Deficit," March 16, 2006. http://bayh.senate.gov.

49. Victor N. Corpus, "Striking the US Where It Hurts," *Asia Times*, October

19, 2006. www.atimes.com.

50. John Murtha, "United States Army Military Readiness," September 13, 2006. www.house.gov.

51. Robert Gates, "DoD News Briefing with Secretary Gates and Under Secretary Jonas from the Pentagon," Department of Defense, February 5, 2007. www.defenselink.mil.

52. Bruce Hoffman, "Al Qaeda's Renaissance, *Los Angeles Times*, February 20, 2007, p. A21.

List of Illustrations

List of Illustrations

Index

About the Author

Stuart A. Kallen is a prolific author who has written more than 200 non-fiction books for children and young adults over the past 20 years. His books have covered countless aspects of human history, culture, and science from the building of the pyramids to the music of the 21st century. Some of his recent titles include *History of World Music*, *Romantic Art*, and *Women of the Civil Rights Movement*. Kallen is also an accomplished singer-songwriter and guitarist in San Diego, California.